Washing Feet

Servant Leadership in the Church

Robert Curry

Washing Feet: Servant Leadership in the Church
©2016 by DeWard Publishing Company, Ltd.
P.O. Box 6259, Chillicothe, Ohio 45601
800.300.9778
www.deward.com

All rights reserved. No portion of this book may be reproduced in any form without written permission from the publisher.

Cover design by Barry Wallace.

The preponderance of Bible quotations are taken from the The Holy Bible, English Standard Version®, copyright © 2001 by Crossway Bibles, a publishing ministry of Good News Publishers. Used by permission. All rights reserved. Any emphasis in Bible quotations is added.

Reasonable care has been taken to trace original sources for any excerpts and quotations appearing in this book and to document such information. For material not in the public domain, fair use standards and practices were followed. Should any attribution be found to be incorrect or incomplete, the publisher welcomes written documentation supporting correction for subsequent printing.

Printed in the United States of America.

ISBN: 978-1-936341-92-4

Dedications And Acknowledgements

This book is dedicated to my father, William Edward Curry, gospel preacher for a half-century and a man whose faith and dedication to the Lord were a positive influence to many. Early in my ministry, he encouraged me to become a teacher and writer.

The book is also dedicated to Dorothy Ann Wingett Curry, my wife of thirty-seven years. Without her, many of my goals would have not been reached. She stood beside me through the ups and downs of ministry, and allowed me to travel around the world to do evangelism and to teach, most of the time while she remained home. She is my very best friend and companion.

I wish to specifically thank Garry Hill for his encouragement in writing this book and his support in my study of leadership, both formally and personally. Garry is my dear friend of more than forty years, my college roommate, the best man at my wedding, and my companion in many interesting experiences around the world.

Contents

Introduction 7

1. Robert Greenleaf And The Servant Leader Model. 27

2. The Biblical Model Of Servant Leadership 57

3. Followership. 78

4. Vision Casting And Mission Statement. 97

5. Strategy And Implementation 126

6. The Reality And Challenge Of Change 158

7. Issues Of Leadership 176

8. Conflict And Resolution 201

Conclusion. 225

Appendix: A Church Growth Program 229

Bibliography 237

Introduction

Research into the field of organizational leadership has rendered a variety of models, perspectives, and methodologies. Within the research, there have emerged a number of approaches to the study of leadership, such as the *trait approach* that systematically studied the qualities of great leadership, the *skills approach* that focused on abilities, the *style approach* that studied leader behavior, and the "situational approach" with its emphasis on how leadership is done within a given situation.[1] A common factor of this research was its leader-centricity, with little or no thought to those who are being led: in other words, the followers.[2] While leadership has been elevated above followership, servant leadership, by implication, necessarily includes the concern of the leader-follower relationship. This makes sense, really, for leaders cannot function alone since they must have at least person to follow them, and followers cannot function alone for they must have a leader to lead them. Servant leadership, in part, expresses the leader-follower dynamic, that each can only function with the cooperation and participation of the other. This is one reason why I believe the servant leadership model offers a foundational approach to proper, effective,

---

[1] Peter G. Northouse, *Leadership: Theory and* Practice, 5th edition (Los Angeles, London, New Dehli: Sage, 2010), 15, 39, 69, 89.

[2] Followership will be discussed in greater detail in chapter two.

biblical congregational leadership, for biblical leadership is about the function of leaders and followers together as they, collectively, follow the greatest leader of all: Jesus Christ.

A variety of leadership models have emerged through the decades, each with a view of how leadership might be accomplished. A few of them are intriguing, for they have had an impact on the focus of this book, servant leadership. Many scholars of leadership would consider them as dominant models of leadership into which the idea of servant leadership might be inserted. I believe that servant leadership is capable of standing on its own when understood and utilized properly, but an understanding other models of leadership can help one grasp elements that are vital to the model of servant leadership.

One of those models is *transformational leadership*, "which gives more attention to the charismatic and affective elements of leadership [with an] emphasis on intrinsic motivation and follower development."[3] Put simply, transformational leadership seeks to transform people, to change them in some effective, positive, and productive way. Transformational leadership is motivational in scope, seeking to bring out in followers more than what is expected. While not intentionally a model of transformational leadership per se, the United States Army's slogan, "Be all that you can be," comes to mind. In fact, the American military as a whole might come to mind as images of the eighteen-year-old high school graduate emerges as a Marine following his experience on Parris Island.

Transformational leadership is not about power, at least not as power is understood and pursued in traditional thinking. The power in transformational leadership is found, in part, in the development of the followers and so the development of the organization as a whole. The transformational leader exercises power, of

---

[3] Northouse, *Leadership*, 171.

course, or he or she cannot be in the lead. Such power, however, is not seen in domination or exploitation, and a separation of the peasants from the nobility, but in the shared ideals of the productivity, effectiveness, and purpose of the organization.

James McGregor Burns, who adopted the concept of transformation as a method of leadership, saw it as the connection of leader and follower where the needs and outlook of both are inseparable.[4] Transformational leadership is not a model associated with the industrial giants such as Rockefeller, Westinghouse, Ford, Vanderbilt, and others who built their empires on the efforts of those who worked for them. This is not the wealthy CEO who stands several stories above the streets below in a plush and expansive office while the laborers struggle to turn a screw, sort the mail, or pull a lever for minimum wage, or less.

A second model is *authentic leadership* which is not as easily described or practiced as it might seem. The idea of and quest for *authenticity* is a relatively new study in social science. In fact, as a theory, authentic leadership is still being assessed and formed as a developing method, so, warns Peter Northouse, it "needs to be considered more tentatively: it is likely to change as new research about the theory is published."[5] As purely a methodological theory of social science, I agree that this is true, but as a component of spiritual servant leadership, I believe it is more

---

[4] Northouse, *Leadership,* 172, citing James McGregor Burns, *Leadership* (New York: Harper and Row), 1978. It should be noted at this point that Burns developed two types of leadership: transactional and transformational. The former was distinguished from the latter in that it emphasized the interaction and exchange between leaders and followers, such as politicians who gain voters through various promises or the managers who promise promotions to the workers for exceeding goals and quotas. Put simply, transactional leadership is about reciprocal exchange, while transformational leadership is about moral engagement and connection through motivation and development. In this book I am not concerned with transactional leadership, so this brief note will suffice to acquaint the reader with the methodological theory.

[5] Ibid., 205.

focused and assessed. I suggest that the Bible proposes authenticity and so authentic leadership.

Consider, for example, Paul's encouragement to Timothy in 2 Timothy 4.1–5:

> I charge you in the presence of God and of Christ Jesus, who is to judge the living and the dead, and by his appearing and his kingdom: preach the word; be ready in season and out of season; reprove, rebuke, and exhort, with complete patience and teaching. For the time is coming when people will not endure sound teaching, but having itching ears they will accumulate for themselves teachers to suit their own passions, and will turn away from listening to the truth and wander off into myths. As for you, always be sober-minded, endure suffering, do the work of an evangelist, fulfill your ministry.

I insist that Paul stressed a sense of spiritual authenticity to his young friend as Timothy sought to minister to the church in Ephesus. In other words, he encouraged Timothy to never abandon who he is as a disciple of Jesus Christ: take every opportunity to preach (only) the word of God; be willing to make a stand for the truth as well as stand with the church as troublesome times are approaching; be mature and in control (sober-minded); be willing to do whatever needs to be done to fulfill his ministry. In other words, be true to the Lord, be true to yourself, and be true to those you serve.[6]

At the risk of stating the obvious, authentic leadership is concerned with the authenticity of leaders and what they do to lead. This definition, however, fails to articulate the actual task of leading authentically. Northouse attempts to define it

---

[6] Other passage related to authenticity and authentic leadership might include Galatians 2.20 and 2 Peter 1.16–21. The greatest expression of authenticity is of course found in the example of Jesus and an account that illustrates it is the temptations of Satan in the wilderness (Matt. 4.1–11; Luke 4.1–13).

through three approaches.[7] First, the intrapersonal definition is concerned with the leader's inner-self: self-knowledge, self-regulation, and self-concept; life-story and experience is significant in this definition. So then, authentic leaders lead by being equipped through their own story and perspectives of their experiences. Second, the developmental definition does not recognize a fixed trait within the leader, but acknowledges and embraces the nurturing of the leader in a developmental way. Through the nurturing of their experiences, such leaders develop a positive outlook and a strong ethic of their task. Third, the interpersonal definition emphasizes the leader-follower relationship and how the purpose and task of the organization is embraced by all involved.

A third model is *team leadership*, where effectiveness and productivity are associated with the role of the leader within a team effort. In this way, the model expresses the leader-follower relationship, but recognizes the leader as a driving force within the team. While similar in scope with transformational leadership, as well as expressing a level of authenticity within the leader, team leadership emphasizes the task of the organization as a process and the leader is understood as a driving, motivational, and stabilizing force within the organization.

Team leadership manifests itself in the way the leader functions within the team:

1. Does he or she supervise or take action/help?
2. Does the leader function best as a motivator or doer?
3. Is the leader's task best understood as relational within the team or as a teacher/trainer for the team?
4. What are the internal and external issues that the team faces?
5. Is the leader a coach, cheerleader, disciplinarian, man-

---

[7] Northouse, *Leadership*, 206–208.

ager, negotiator, networker, maintainer, or all of the above (and more)?

It is the opinion of this writer that servant leadership can be understood through the components of transformation, authenticity, and team-mindedness. Others may have a different approach to the servant model, any of those I have mentioned, as well as a number of other components. The thesis of this book, however, is an examination of the servant leader model and I believe it is best represented through foundational and functional components that seek to be transformational, that emerge from a leader who seeks authenticity in himself and his methods of leadership, and that is servant-follower and team oriented.

The research and assessment of the servant leadership model is still relatively young. The ongoing research has been limited primarily to the business world, and then applied as well in other fields of social science such as the political and military world. Some, but relatively little, research and study has been devoted to how this model serves the religious/ecclesial world; that is not to say that no research has been done, but what has been done is limited, to be sure. I am of the opinion that the servant leadership model fits well into religious/ecclesial concerns.

Over the past few decades, several social and communicative concerns were introduced into the research to determine how they address a variety of cooperative issues that may or may not have been avoided in former leader-centric studies. Within this research also emerged a conscious appraisal of the moral component of leadership, especially within the transformational and authentic leadership models.[8] Out of this school of thought has come a greater awareness of the leader as a servant to those he or she

---

[8] I will not examine transformational, team, and authentic leadership as separate models in this book, but they will be concepts woven into the fabric of servant leadership.

leads. These ethical, moral, human, and relational concerns form a legitimate foundation upon which the servant leader model is placed. Those concerns are biblical, as well.

Some Preliminary Thoughts

I have been preaching the gospel for almost forty years and have had a variety of ministry experiences: good, bad, and somewhere in between, as is the case with any endeavor. I believe I can safely say that each of these experiences were due to, in part at least, the input of those in a position of leadership. In each and every positive experience, the constructive contributions of the leaders emerged from their desire to be first, servants, and second, leaders, and so servant leaders. In each and every negative experience, the destructive contributions of the leaders emerged from their lack of concern for or knowledge of the task of leadership, and so servant leadership. That statement is not entirely fair, however, for whether the experience was positive, negative, or somewhere in between, the leaders were not the only cause. In each of these experiences, it was also those who were being led, the followers, who contributed to the end result.

The study of leadership includes a wide variety of social, communicative, motivational, persuasive, and educational concerns. In a consideration of congregational, spiritual leadership, there are those concerns, as well as questions of scripturality, spiritualiy, theology, ethics, and morality. Since these components of leadership and its dynamics are known, why then is the actual praxis of leadership, and more specifically for this book, congregational leadership, such a problem? In the same way, why is followership a problem? Why is the organization that is the congregation too often less than successful?

Leadership must be a concern of every congregation and its leadership; not merely men who *assume* the task of leadership, but who *understand* the task of leadership as well. If the subject of leadership is to make contact with congregational studies, a clear path into theological and biblical concerns must be understood. Why? Leadership is a biblical study!

Don Howell wrote in the introduction to his book, *Servants of the Servant*:

> Leadership is a concept of immense importance, one that has gained increasing visibility in the past two decades. The number of books, monographs, journal articles and even doctoral dissertations devoted to some aspect of leadership is staggering. There has been almost exponential growth in the number of seminars offered to help people develop as leaders and to nurture their skills in training others. If one does a search of *amazon.com* for books with the term 'leader' or 'leadership' in the title, the number of entries that come up are 1,902 and 4,628 respectively. When one expands the search to 'leadership' as the subject or category of the book, 10,244 entries are available to scroll through. Clearly those in political, corporate, educational, and ecclesiastical worlds are looking for help as to how to effectively lead others and they are getting an abundance of advice. Countries, companies and churches rise and fall with the quality of their leadership. Over the past twenty-five years in vocational Christian ministry, primarily a church planter and theological educator, this writer has encountered numerous examples of both constructive as well as unhealthy patterns of leadership. What has stood out is that effective leadership is critical to the success of any organization or group in accomplishing its mission.[9]

This introductory statement sets the bar for what the study of leadership must be: (1) leadership's increasing focus as a viable topic of research and writing, (2) its place in organizational development, and (3) its place in church and ministry studies. Howell's

---

[9] Don N. Howell, *Servants of the Servant: A Biblical Theology of Leadership* (Eugene, OR: Wipf & Stock, Publishers, 2003), 1.

book is an excellent study of the biblical case for effective leadership, by those who would choose to carry out such a monumental task as servants to Jesus Christ.

As a student of organizational leadership, both formerly and in personal study, I related on a number of levels with Howell's observations of leadership. First, I too have marveled at the ever-growing supply of literature and lectures discussing the place and function of leadership in a congregational setting. Being formulated prior to 2003, Howell's estimation of some 1,902 books with "leader" and 4,628 with "leadership" in the title respectively, as well as 10,244 with "leadership" as the subject, ten years before this writer constructed this book, falls short of the plethora of titles and lectures now available.

Second, after more than three-and-a-half decades of congregational ministry, as well as experience as a lecturer and instructor of ministry, theology, textual studies, and leadership, I too have seen my share of both effective and ineffective, even horrendous, leadership within the congregations of the churches of Christ.[10] As I will address further on, poor, ineffective, and even destructive leadership appears to far outweigh its much more admirable counterpart.

A Note of Concern

I do not know what it will be like in eternity with God—no mortal can know—but imagine the opportunity to ask the Lord

---

[10] The foundational framework of this book is focused on the churches of Christ which accepts congregational leadership under the autonomous authority of a plurality of men who are designated "elders" or "shepherds," based upon the use of *episkopos* and *presbuteros* in the Greek New Testament. The term "pastor" within the churches of Christ does not indicate the preacher/minister, but the elders. This writer understands and respects the pastorate assumed by other bodies of American Christianity and, through discussion with others, recognizes a commonality of rejoicing in the presence of good leadership, as well as frustration in the presence of its less-than-effective counterpart.

questions regarding topics of interest. I seriously doubt such will be the case, for the cares and concerns of this world will no longer be of any consequence. However, for the sake of making a point, if such an experience would occur, one of the questions I would like to ask is what the Lord had in mind when orchestrating the plan for autonomous leadership within the congregations. Somehow we seem to have missed it; we are just off target in a few cases and not even in the neighborhood with many other cases through the church as a whole. There is just too much uncertainty.

Congregations around the country, as well as throughout the world, are blessed to have dedicated, effective men who shepherd them. They lead their congregations through a devotion to the Lord, a desire for biblical knowledge and spiritual growth, and a sense of purpose. Is it fair to say such leaders are the exception; that more congregational leaders have little knowledge of what their task is and how it should be done? Perhaps, perhaps not; it probably depends on who you ask and their perspective on the subject.

I talk to a lot of my peers and colleagues and I know is that there are many preachers, this preacher included, ministry staff, and office staff who are more than frustrated with what they consider bad and ineffective leadership.[11] Almost every preacher or member of the ministry staff has his accounts of ill treatment, poor communication, unrealistic expectations, and so on. My father, a Gospel preacher for fifty years, told me very early in my career, "You will never be treated better or worse than how you

---

[11] I have no intention whatsoever to sound overly critical or mean. Shepherds, as well as all conscientious leaders have a daunting task that far too often goes unappreciated and unrecognized. My point is an apparent and all too common disconnect between the elders, and the ministry and office staff. While examples of less-than-ideal leadership exist, elders all over the country and the world seek to be the men the Lord has commanded them to be and deserve the support of the congregations they serve.

will be treated by the members of the church." It did not take very long for me to realize that my father was right.

Poor, inconsistent, and inappropriate leadership affects the work of the church, and can affect the church's reputation within the community. Consider Paul's admonition to Timothy and the Ephesian church in 1 Timothy 3.1–7. Paul insisted that "an overseer must be above reproach" (2), "respectable" (2), and "well thought of by outsiders" (7). Paul was keenly aware of the delicate and essential reputation of congregational leaders; that they must maintain themselves as leaders with integrity, decency, responsibility, and morality with the needs and concerns of the congregation in mind; in other words, as I will reveal in this book, servant leaders.

Paul also said that the work of an elder is "a good work" (NKJV), a "noble task" (ESV). Why is the task of the congregational shepherd "good" or "noble"? We must realize that Paul stressed such a work as the responsibility of an "overseer," "the role of watching over the congregation."[12] The author of the *Epistles to the Hebrews* wrote, "Obey your leaders and submit to them, for they are keeping watch over your souls, as those who will have to give an account" (Heb. 13.17 ESV). So then, congregational leaders have the good or noble task of being the watchful guardians of the congregation, which is a task of the literal shepherd according to Jesus (cf. John 10.1–21). Luke recorded the instructions of Paul to the elders of the Ephesian church, "Pay careful attention to yourselves and to all the flock, in which the Holy Spirit has made you overseers, to care for the church of God, which he obtained with his own blood" (Acts 20.28).[13]

So yes, it is fair for me, or anyone else for that matter, to insist

---

[12] *ESV Study Bible* (Wheaton, IL: Crossway Bibles, 2008), 2329.

[13] All scripture references and quotations are from the English Standard Version unless otherwise noted.

that strong and appropriate leadership is essential to the identity of a congregational leader. If for no other reason, poor leadership reflects upon the church and its place and function within the community. Elders and preachers all across the country and throughout the world know of cases where congregations have undergone serious, even critical, damage control due to inappropriate behavior, either by the elders themselves or someone else within the congregations they serve and lead. My own career in ministry has included assisting in the rebuilding of congregations after some level of difficulty. We would love to believe that the activities of our congregations go unnoticed unless we desire to reach out into the community; that if something unseemly, unfortunate, and/or inappropriate occurs, it is handled entirely internally. That is not the case, however, especially in a smaller, more tightly knit community where the activities of any organization rarely, if ever, go unnoticed and are too often accentuated in a very negative way through rumor and speculation.

Why Study Leadership In A Church Setting?

This book is about leadership and the application of servant leadership in a congregational setting. It is the result of years of observing congregational leadership from within the overall task of ministry and how such leadership falls somewhere between superior and poor. How then does leadership come to fail, or succeed? What are the assets and the barriers to effective leadership?

What does effective leadership look like and how is it done? While the primary focus of this book is the work of the elders as the spiritual leaders of a congregation, it is not intended to target only the elders; the ministry staff, the deacons, the Bible school teachers, and some, but not all, members within a congregation are also included. The act of leadership is not only done by an eldership, but, in one way or another, it is done at every level of a congregation's work. As the elders shepherd a congregation, they delegate[14] individuals to then take the lead in the implementation of all the congregation will seek to accomplish. I also believe it is essential and helpful for all members of the congregation, especially those who will take some leadership role, to realize what leadership is and the task the elders must faithfully embrace.

The study of spiritual/congregational leadership is relatively new to the churches of Christ, but it has been a topic of importance for many years within the larger religious world. This is not to say that leadership has not been addressed within the churches of Christ, for indeed it has, but the issue has been normally rather narrow in scope, limited mostly to examinations of 1Timothy 3, Titus 1 and, perhaps, Acts 20 as well. While that is all well and good, and certainly necessary, the subject is much larger than a study of those biblical texts. Leadership is a topic within a study of Moses and the Exodus, the work of rebuilding and renewal of Nehemiah and Ezra, and through the experiences of dozens of other biblical characters such as Joseph, Moses, David, and, of course, Jesus; there is no greater example of effective leadership than in the life and ministry of our Lord. In addition to the biblical narratives and historical accounts, one can see the components of leadership in the concepts, words and phrases throughout the biblical text: Jesus' mentoring, equipping and the empowerment of his followers; Solomon's sage advice to his "son;" the historical accounts and conquest.

Within the past couple of decades, perhaps longer, the study of congregational leadership has broadened into something on a much larger and grander scale. Organizational studies, social science, systems theories, congregational research, and leadership theories from the secular world have been incorporated into the

---

[14] Delegation will be discussed further on as an effective tool of leadership.

study of leadership within the congregation. Issues such as spiritual formation and renewal, strategic thinking, cultural intelligence, conflict management, vision and mission, contingencies, and assessment tools have formed a grid of understanding and a formula for action within the task of congregational leadership.

I believe there are two reasons why leadership studies have been avoided by many congregations of the churches of Christ. (The exception to a lack of study would be the occasional elders' workshop or a lesson in a school's lectureship program. Even when such opportunities are available, those who attend, unless their participation is mandatory, are a distinctive minority.)

First, leadership studies are avoided because some, perhaps many, feel there is no need for special consideration of and/or training in leadership. Among conservative and even some moderate congregational leaders, there is perhaps a resistance to seminars and workshops in leadership techniques and related topics due, in part, to stubbornness toward the need for and the process of any formal learning experience, as well as any opportunities for personal and practical growth. For far too many elders, there is simply no need to formally study and learn how to lead a congregation.

Leadership theory is assumed by many to be only fitted for business, education, and political studies. Congregational leadership—which is done within the churches of Christ through the efforts of an autonomous plurality of elders—is not informed by secular concerns (i.e. leadership theory), but only by the Bible. If the Bible is the whole counsel of God, they might insist, why would any other source of information and methods of learning be necessary? To be honest, I agree with this assessment, up to a point. All concerns of church practice and function are to be biblically-oriented, biblically-based, and biblically-governed; nothing in this regard should be founded upon and governed within secular considerations alone. It is the Bible, however, that provides a solid foundation and an efficient learning platform for understanding the theory and practice of effective leadership. Many (dare I say most) of the secular theories of leadership praxis find firm footing within the Bible, especially the theme of this book, servant leadership.

A second reason I feel leadership studies are avoided is because it is assumed so much of the material related to leadership and the practices contained therein is aimed toward congregations that function within the jurisdiction of a synod, diocese, conference, or association, which is something not practiced within the churches of Christ. Such ecclesial[15] governance, they might insist, focuses on leadership through a plurality of levels where the energy of leadership moves up and down those levels (i.e. executive management, middle-level management, regional management, appointed committees, congregational pastorates, and lay-leader functions). So then, much—if not all—of the leadership material available, they might assume, focuses on church settings and issues associated only with a multi-level ecclesial type of governance.

The first reason is connected to the second—that leadership does not need to be studied because it is oriented outside of the purview of the churches of Christ. I believe this is a misinformed view. It is true that the majority of the material on leadership and its related topics are written by and published for churches separate from the churches of Christ. It is also true that a significant segment of the literature addresses the function and place of the pastor/preacher/leader (rather than the preacher working under the authority of an eldership), the work and responsibilities

---

[15] The term "ecclesial" or "ecclesiastical" refers to what is associated with and assumed to be the larger concerns of a church.

of corporate governing organizational boards, and a number of other concerns that are not a part of the practices of the churches of Christ. The amount of material that is written by members of the churches of Christ[16] is minimal. That does not mean, however, that there is not good material available from among us. Some examples would include the following:

1. Lynn Anderson, *They Smell Like Sheep: Spiritual Leadership for the 21st Century* (West Monroe, LA: Howard Publishing Co.), 1997.
2. Michael C. Armour and Don Browning, *Systems-Sensitive Leadership: Empowering Diversity Without Polarizing the Church* (Joplin, MO: College Press), 1995.
3. Ian A. Fair, *Leadership in the Kingdom: Sensitive Strategies for the Church in a Changing World* (Abilene, TX: ACU Press), 1996.
4. Norman Hogan, *Leadership in the Local Church* (Henderson, TN: Nakari Publications), 1988.

This is an incomplete listing, of course, but it gives the reader an idea of what is available.

The actual concept of leadership study should be a concern of the churches of Christ, but that has not been predominately the case. It has been embraced more so among churches other than the churches of Christ, and that is unfortunate. Due to its greater emphasis within church groups other than the churches of Christ,

---

[16] In using the term "churches of Christ" I am primarily referring to the non-instrumental churches of Christ. For the purpose of inclusivity regarding the broader concerns within the thesis of this book, I am also thinking of the instrumental churches of Christ as well as the conservative and some moderate Christian churches. While these "Restoration churches" have practical differences (e.g. mechanical instruments of music in worship), that discussion is not the purview of this book. The purview of this book is congregational leadership and its dynamics, and is founded upon what this author views as the Scriptural practice of an autonomous body of shepherds/elders rather than an ecclesial headquarters or exclusive pastorate.

leadership dynamics are too often viewed as a *denominational* study, fitted primarily for only *denominational* concerns. I submit that the study is biblical, and so then legitimate. I also believe that our attitude, that of the churches of Christ, toward the study of leadership theory, methodology, and function needs to change.

Through a much wider lens, the numbers of books that are legitimate for understanding congregational leadership or some aspect of it are numerous.[17] Some are written from a perspective respecting autonomy and a plurality of elders, while others write from a clergy/pastorate perspective. I feel that most, if not all, have at least something to offer, regardless of the theological background and inclinations of the author.

When one visits a good cafeteria, he will always find things he does not like, but there is always plenty still to eat. In the same way, one can usually, if not always, find some useable nugget of information in the variety of books available, even though much of any given book moves in a direction different than one's own. I recall visiting a used book store many years ago and finding a wide variety of books associated with the broader view of leadership, ministry, and theology. Each of the books were priced anywhere from a dollar to ten dollars. I walked out with an entire box of books. Many of them were written by men who do not share my own theological and biblical views. I found, however, that even though this was the case, there was that chapter, that section, that paragraph, or that sentence that expressed a profitable observation, thought, and/or idea. Certainly that was worthy paying a few dollars.

So then, regardless of the theological and doctrinal foundation, each book offers at least a morsel for one's spiritual palate. For example, one might take advice on project planning within a church board and implement it as project planning within the eldership, for a deacon's meeting, or a Vacation Bible School com-

---

[17] Refer to the bibliography.

mittee. For another example, one might take material regarding the role of the "pastor" in implementing change and adapt it to the role of the elders in adapting change. As a final example, information on liturgical[18] issues can be taken from their denominational constructs and implemented for more effective worship within the churches of Christ, even if the material reflects philosophical rather than practical connections. In other words, something good can be found in almost any source.

So I ask the question again: Why study congregational leadership? I propose three reasons. First, the study of congregational leadership will make the men who serve as the church's eldership better motivators, planners, and problem solvers. Unless an elder is specifically trained and experienced in functioning as an organizational leader (e.g. corporate, educational, or factory administration), he will be unfamiliar with the concerns and problems of leading an organization.[19] Too many problems that arise within a congregation cause more trouble than necessary simply because leaders do not know what to do to find a resolution. I will examine the task and challenge of resolution (e.g. conflict resolution, implementation resolution, and contingency resolution) later in the book.

Second, if people other than the elders are aware of leadership practices and issues, they can become better workers, for they will have an understanding of what it means for the elders to lead (shepherd) and what it takes for the workers to implement effectively that which the elders decide. A significant concept within (organizational) leadership theory studies is leadership-followership, and making the congregation aware of the issues and prac-

---

[18] According to *Webster's New Collegiate Dictionary* Springfield, MA: G & C Merriam Company, 1973) 673, "liturgy" can be defined as, "a rite or body of rites prescribed for public worship."

[19] One of the ways of understanding and building a congregation is to see it as systematic organization with many layers of social, emotional, and practical concerns, as well as human, financial, and physical resources.

tices of leadership is a key component of follower studies. I will also address this in much greater detail later in the book.

Third, the study of congregational leadership will allow the eldership to see the congregation as a fluid, functional, and changing system of emotions, needs, and perspectives that must be carefully, prayerfully, and effectively managed. Congregational populations rise and fall due to how these issues, as well as other issues, are addressed. This is a critical component of effective leadership that I will also discuss later in the book.

Is the study of leadership absolutely essential for congregations to remain faithful and spiritually effective? Will a congregation fail if its leaders do not engage in leadership study? No, for churches have existed for decades without ever engaging in the study of leadership. The study of congregational leadership and all that goes with it will never be a "cure-all" or "magic pill" for the needs of any congregation. As I will discuss later, no theory of man alone will be enough to insure success in spiritual matters. The theories of man, such as the organizational model of servant leadership, must function only as tools of a foundational biblical spirituality.

What a study of congregational leadership can potentially do is equip the elders and those they designate for duty to know how to develop faith, utilize talents, encourage moral goodness, and spiritually form the congregation. They can potentially also come know what it means to empower the congregation, equip them with the spiritual tools to do the work, embrace the challenges, enable the membership, effectively strategize, build and tear down, and resolve to improve, all of which I will discuss in this book.

A Disclaimer

A final note before I begin. I am not an elder, nor have I ever been one. For many men who serve as elders, my not being *among them* might lead to an automatic dismissal of any controversial premise, any seemingly negative comment, and any type of advice I will offer. I understand; I really do understand. I too, if I were in their role as elders, would question the right or place of someone with no eldership experience who appears to second-guess and question their daunting task. I have no intention whatsoever to sound critical or mean.

My purpose in this book is to offer observations, perspectives, and pertinent information regarding the dynamics of leadership, especially servant leadership, and to observe how the task of congregation leadership is done biblically, and therefore effectively, as servant leaders. The day may come when I will have the privilege of serving as an elder within the churches of Christ. If and when that happens, I want to be as prepared as possible, assuming my role in that level of congregational leadership in a biblical, practical, and effective manner.

So then, I did not write this book as an elder. I wrote this book, first, as an experienced leader in ministry, Christian education, evangelism, and missions. Second, I wrote this book based on formal and informal education in both organizational and congregational leadership.[20] Third, I wrote this book following research in both organizational and congregational leadership dynamics and praxis, and the direct and indirect input of elders among the churches of Christ throughout the country.[21]

---

[20] While the primary focus of this book is the eldership, I am not isolating "leadership" to the elders only, but to anyone who assumes a leadership role, under the servant leadership of the elders, in ministry, education, and evangelism, as well as practical and physical duties.

[21] The input from elders began to inform my research more than three decades ago—I had no plans to write a book on congregational leadership until just a few years ago—through successive question and answer experiences, formal and informal questionnaires, and conversations with elders regarding their leadership philosophies, victories and defeats, frustrations, likes and dislikes, experiences, vision-casting and mission statements, and personal observations.

ONE | *Robert Greenleaf and the Servant Leader Model*

The concept of servant leadership was placed into the public forum in the 1970s by the late Sydney Greenleaf,[1] who wrote from a business perspective and included other forms of leadership, primarily educational and religious. While by no means a dominant thesis of his model, his discussion of religious/spiritual/church leadership is valuable. It includes issues of faith and ethics, as well the role of churches in the larger national and global community. His inclusion of churches and their place within the discussion of leadership is not theological, not even textual, really, for he does not take time to evaluate biblical models or theological constructs. He writes as a believer, both of the organization and churches as organizational models, realizing that church leadership must be considered in the larger discussion of organizational leadership.[2]

Greenleaf brought to light the revolutionary idea that leaders are to be servants as well, that their role is not to dominate, but to lead through example and humility with the welfare of the larger organization and those they lead being a primary concern.

---

[1] R. K. Greenleaf, *Servant leadership: A journey into the nature of legitimate power and greatness* (New York: Paulist Press), 1977.

[2] Ibid. See chapter 7: "Servant Leadership in Churches," 231–261.

N. Nayab wrote:

> The major strength of servant leadership theory is its contribution to organizational development. The servant leader deviates from the traditional leadership style of dominating subordinates and telling them what to do, and rather empowers subordinates and inspires them to perform. The servant [leader] acts proactively to set the way, and inspire the subordinates to follow. Such inspiration leads to collective efforts, the results of which turn out to be more than the sum of individual parts.[3]

Since Greenleaf introduced the world to the concept of servant leadership, many have followed his path, developing and adapting the model to function effectively within other leadership fields (e.g., spiritual, military, and education), as well as the larger concerns of organizational leadership as a grid that may or may not be laid over one or more of those models.[4] So then, servant leadership has been peer reviewed, scrutinized, studied, and tested since its inception.

Greenleaf's Servant Leadership Model

The concept of servant leadership has been a topic of discussion from a few decades ago and into the present time. This "paradoxical approach to leadership" has been expressed through its "strong altruistic ethical overtones" that a leader must be concerned for

---

[3] Nayab, N. Edited by Ginny Edwards. "Servant Leadership- Strengths and Weaknesses." May 5, 2011.

[4] Organizational leadership theory is not something that can necessarily be laid as a grid over any given leadership model. In other words, organizational leadership is not the umbrella model under which all other models are laid. For example, organizational and educational leadership theory are different models in a number of ways. That is not to say that educational institutions cannot or should not be understood as organizations (the same can be said of congregations, military facilities, corporations, political units, and so on).

the followers by caring for and nurturing them.[5] Such care and nurture is essential to the servant model of leadership. Greenleaf adopted the idea of servant leadership after reading Hesse's (1956) *Journey to the East,* which emphasized the great leader who must first be a servant leader, for "that simple fact is the key to his greatness."[6] The character at the center of the story is Leo, "who accompanies the party as the servant who does their menial chores, but whom also sustains them with his spirit and his song."[7] Leo emerged not only as the sustainer of the journey, but also the epitome of the powerful leader who internalizes the responsibility of leadership and, more specifically, the joy offered up by a leader "who ostensibly served only in menial ways but who, by the quality of his inner life that was manifest in his presence, lifted others up and made the journey possible."[8]

Greenleaf's thesis was revolutionary, "a new leadership philosophy,"[9] for leadership models that emphasize leader-centricity as well as servant-centricity appear to be opposed to one another. J. Laub offered a glimpse of the tension: "There is a confusion of terms, to be sure. We talk about servant leadership as if it is leadership."[10] Greenleaf, however, sought to bridge the gap between these two models, so apparently far apart, by insisting that the leader who is also a servant will "make sure that other

---

[5] Northouse, Leadership, 384–385.

[6] Greenleaf, *Servant Leadership,* 21.

[7] Ibid.

[8] Ibid., 57–58.

[9] J. E. Barbuto & D. W. Wheeler, (2006), Scale development and construct clarification of servant leadership. Group & Organization Management 31(1), 300–326. doi: 10.1177/1059601106287091, p. 301.

[10] J. Laub (2004, August), "Defining servant leadership: A recommended typology for servant leadership studies." Paper session presented at the Servant Leadership Roundtable, Regent University, 4.

people's highest priority needs are being served."[11] Laub insisted that servant leadership seeks to value and develop people by building community, practicing authenticity, and displaying leadership for the good of followers. In this way, Laub adds, servant leaders share power and status that supports the good of each individual follower, the organization as a whole, and all who are served by the organization.

Indeed, Greenleaf's model of leading as a servant was and is revolutionary; it is also difficult to fathom if the two concepts cannot be enmeshed. In other words, the idea of a servant as a leader, or a leader as a servant, will not work if either side—leader and servant—cannot imagine both existing effectively within each. This is especially true, more so perhaps within the mentality of a leader if that leader refuses to understand and embrace the identity of a true servant; even more so when one considers the biblical leader-servant model, which I will discuss later.

Greenleaf built a case for the servant-leadership model in almost every aspect of human work and interaction: (a) business, (b) education, (c) foundations, (d) churches, and (e) the world. He insisted that this must be done because of the community of all humanity. He wrote:

> One is asked, then, to accept the human condition, its sufferings and its joys, and to work with its imperfections as the foundation upon which the individual will build wholeness through adventurous creative achievement. For the person with creative potential there is no wholeness except in using it. . . .And, as I ponder the fusing of servant and leader, it seems a dangerous creation: dangerous for the natural servant to become a leader, dangerous for the leader to be servant first, and dangerous for the follower to insist on being led by a servant.[12]

---

[11] Greenleaf, *Servant Leadership*, 27.

[12] Ibid., 26.

Indeed, Greenleaf's "fusing of servant and leader" is "a dangerous creation" if the leader will not accept his role as a servant as well.

Greenleaf admitted facing two problems as he developed the idea of servant leadership. First, the idea for a leader who is also a servant did not emerge from "conscious logic" but from Hesse's character, Leo, and Greenleaf did not see that the question was one to be answered from "a logical progression from premise to conclusion. Rather, I see it as fragments of data to be fed into my internal computer from which intuitive insights come."[13] In this way, servant leadership has been seen as an internal practice, something from the inside, and not something that is based merely on hard data or productivity. In other words, a leader who is a servant does not respond merely with the intention of something measureable on a data sheet, growth chart, or financial bottom line, but functions from a motivation that comes from within. Greenleaf introduced a leadership model that emerged out of the data-centric corporate world, but functioned as an intuitive reaction from the heart.

The second problem Greenleaf acknowledged was that as there were contradictions in his idea of a servant as a leader, so there were contradictions in his world: (a) order, chaos, and creation, (b) individualism within community, and (c) the comfort and dismay of reason and intuition. He concluded, "My resolution of these two problems is to offer the relevant gleanings of my experience in the form of a series of unconnected little essays, some developed more fully than others, with the suggestion that they be read and pondered separately within the context of this opening section."[14] In Greenleaf's mind, due to the human condition and the needs of the world community, it would be the servant-leader who would bring positive change. So he wrote:

---

[13] Ibid.

[14] Ibid., 27.

Servants, by definition, are fully human. Servant-leaders are functionally superior because they are closer to the ground—they hear things, see things, know things, and their intuitive insight is exceptional. Because of this they are dependable and trusted. They know the meaning of that line from Shakespeare's sonnet, "They that have power to hurt and will do none...."[15]

One can see the controversial nature of Greenleaf's conclusions, that the servant leader is presumably "functionally superior" to other leaders who do not serve those they lead, but embrace an authoritative, domineering style of leadership. If the servant-leader is dependable and socially aware, then does Greenleaf, by contrast, assume those who are not servant-leaders are not as dependable and socially aware? If so, the model of servant leadership emerges superior to others because of its emphasis on the leader-follower relationship. It is humanity that separates this model from others.

There is indeed a real-world, or better yet, a more-effective-world, point to be made from this. Greenleaf insisted that servant leaders are "functionally superior," which sounds restrictive, even arrogant, to be sure. His point, however, is that leaders who function from the mind-set of a servant allow the human element to exist within the task of leadership. In other words, leaders who are also servants function on levels including but also beyond the bottom line; they function with an awareness of the human element and their place within it. In this way leaders are aware of how they interact rather than react; how they assimilate, share, empower, and equip those they both lead as well as serve. Instead of only being concerned with the bottom line of the organization, they are concerned with the members of the organization, which includes them.

---

[15] Ibid., 56.

Assessment Of The Servant Leadership Model

Even though it is prominent in the field of leadership theory, and gaining ground, servant leadership is not as well researched as other leadership models.[16] Sharon Drury wrote, "Servant leadership remains an intuitive-based theory because little empirical (observable; testable as experienced) evidence of servant-leader behavior exists."[17] This is a problem if servant leadership is to be viewed as a viable method. Does this lack of empirical evidence affect the use of a servant leader model in a congregational setting? Yes, it does, if we are seeking a model that is recognized within the general world of leadership studies. On the other hand, no, it does not really matter if we are seeking a model of leadership that is definable biblically. I will address this in more detail later.

Laub insisted, "Writers on servant leadership have not taken the time or the precision of effort to clearly define the concepts they are working with. How can we research something that we have not defined? How can we effectively explore and then present a concept that remains vague and anecdotal.[18] As a construct, much of the research has been to compare servant leadership to other models, such as the research of Sen Sendjaya, James Sorros, and J.C. Santora (2008), where it was compared for its similarities and differences with transformational, authentic, and spiritual leadership. John Barbuto and Daniel Wheeler (2006) noticed its distinctiveness apart from charismatic and transformational leadership, its biblical, religious, and spiritual articulations, and its contrast to the trait, behavioral, and contingency approaches to leadership.

---

[16] Bass & Bass, 2008.

[17] Sharon Drury, *Handbook of Leadership for Church Leaders* (Regent University, 2003), 21.

[18] Laub, "Defining Servant Leadership," 13.

So then, not only has it been less researched than other models of leadership, but a significant portion of the research has been only to compare and contrast it to the other models and that have weakened its impact and acceptability. While its profile has increased in recent years, servant leadership still lacks clarity, for most of its identity is found within the task of being a servant and not a leader. What is needed in the research and the results of its use is a greater understanding of how a leader can be a servant.

Laub referred to servant leadership as an "emerging sub-field of leadership study."[19]

While all of the research in recent years has been helpful in determining the validity and functionality of the servant leadership model, more needs to be done to establish its legitimate place as a model of organizational leadership.

Is servant leadership merely a sub-field of other, more valid models? In other words, is servant leadership only viable if it is understood merely as part of a larger leadership dynamic? If servant leadership is a legitimate model capable of standing on its own, is it leadership or management? In addition, is it servant-centric or follower-centric?[20] Laub wrote that servant leadership is "a mindset, a paradigm, and a way of leading, a subset of leadership. It is a way of engaging in an intentional change process through which leaders and followers, joined by a shared purpose, initiate action to pursue a common vision."[21] While much is still unexplored and undetermined, there is much to be discovered as the paradigm continues to be researched. Servant leadership has the potential to be an effective and efficient model of leadership due to its emphasis of followership, authenticity, transformation, and ethical behavior.

---

[19] Laub, "Defining Servant Leadership," 2.

[20] Ibid.

[21] Ibid., 19.

The gap in the research notwithstanding, some progress has been made to determine what servant leadership, as a distinct and individual model, really is. Put simply, it is leadership by those who are servants by nature.[22] Significant to the discussion are the identifying traits of servant leaders and the key components of how servant leadership is done. Several[23] have summarized servant leadership according to its key components and each summary has been relatively the same. The list, of course, is long, so I will list three of what I consider to be the more foundational traits.

Humility

The first foundational, essential trait that emerges for me is humility, which is often misunderstood, misapplied, and undefined. An article in *Harvard Business Review* puts it simply and succinctly in the title: "The Best Leaders are Humble Leaders."[24] The servant leader exhibits the characteristic of humility, but it is difficult for some leaders to feel and display humility. This can be the result of several causes: (1) a sense of entitlement because of the position he or she holds; (2) the admiration and adulation of those being led; (3) the possession of power inherent in the task of servant leadership.

Humility must be associated with leadership, however, for the expectations and duties of the task will lead the servant leader to realize he has much still to learn and do. People who pursue higher levels of education and experience will perhaps come to this realization. As they are stretched and reshaped academically to think and process information in new ways, learning to color out-

---

[22] Northouse, *Leadership*, 385.

[23] For example, Bass & Bass, 2008 and Barbuto & Wheeler, 2006.

[24] Jeanie Prime and Elizabeth Salib, "The Best Leaders are Humble Leaders," May 12, 2014. *Harvard Business Review*. http://hbr.org/2014/05/the-best-leaders-are-humble-leaders, p. 1.

side the lines, as it were, and crossing perceived boundaries and proposed limitations that they assumed earlier in their education, they come to embrace the wealth of knowledge and experience available to them, and what they still have not obtained. In this way, the servant leader comes to realize that the world is much bigger than he assumed, the well into which he casts his bucket is much deeper than he ever knew, and he begins to embrace his need to stretch and grow.

Humility is too often misunderstood. Sometimes it is assumed that humility is something self-effacing and self-denying; that it is not self-confident and exudes little or no power and authority. I believe humility is exactly the opposite. One can be humble in attitude and conduct, but still display authority, power, control, and confidence, for those are necessary components of leadership. Humility, however, recognizes the role of the leader as a guide, visionary, mover, and shaker, as well, which demands a consideration of how those who are led will be equipped and empowered for action. In other words, the humble servant leader must be confident that he is up to the task, demonstrating authority and power as he recognizes that it is not about him, but about the group, the organization, the congregation. Leaders are humble enough to realize that the task and the good of the organization are much bigger than they.

So, what does it mean to lead, as a servant, through humility? Aubrey Malphurs put it simply, but concisely: "Servant leaders lead with humility. Matthew 20.25–26 says, 'Jesus called them together and said, "You know that the rulers of the Gentiles lord it over them, and their high officials exercise authority over them. Not so with you."' Jesus teaches that servant leaders lead humbly. They are characterized as humble or selfless leaders. Thus a critical element of your leadership is how you serve. It is about your humility, not ego."²⁵ Laub wrote, "Servant leadership is an understanding and practice of leadership that places the good of those led over the self-interest of the leader."²⁶ So, first, the humble servant leader must seek to know and attend to the presence and function of others within the organization, and so then, for the purposes of this book, the church. This manifests itself in a number of ways, but I will suggest three. First, the humble servant leader includes the observations and opinions of others.

This is an essential element of effective servant leadership but, sadly, it is too often ignored in an organization and, even more sadly, within the church. I recall an eldership from many years ago who felt that the only ones to ascertain the needs and direction of their congregation were themselves, without any input from others. While elders must assume their authority to shepherd, oversee, and manage the flock (cf. Acts 20.28; 1 Tim. 3.4; et al.), it is a mistake to not take advantage of the insight, perspectives, and observations of those they shepherd, and so serve. I will address this in greater detail later in the book, but I will point out here that elders have at their disposal members of the congregation with the experience, education, and integrity to see what they (elders) do not see, to know what they do not know, and accomplish what they cannot accomplish on their own. Humble servant leaders will be wise to seek the input of others, including and especially, perhaps, those within the congregation they shepherd.

Second, humble servant leaders will make sure the needs of their congregation are being met. In organizational dynamics, this lies within the concern of *team performance*. The concept of a *team* applies also to the work of a congregation of the Lord's church, as well, for an effective congregation will seek to work

---

²⁵ Aubrey Malphurs, *Being leaders: The Nature of Authentic Christian Leadership* (Grand Rapids, MI: Baker Books, 2003), 34.

²⁶ Laub, 17.

together to accomplish its tasks and reach its goals. I will address this, too, later in the book. This task of humble servant leaders is a part of creating an environment of effective performance (work). Do not misunderstand, however, for I am not referring to so-called "needs-oriented" ministry (i.e. adapting the work, function, and practice of the congregation to "felt needs" or personal agendas). I am referring, instead, to the individual and collective needs of the congregation as an assembly of human beings seeking greater spiritual growth and Christian practice. Humble servant leaders will do well to be aware and understanding of the needs of the flock.

Third, it is imperative that humble servant leaders, once they have received the input and have become aware of the needs of the congregation, will allow the congregation to take their place within the work of that congregation, and then allow them to function as best they can. Micro-managing is a fruitless, suffocating practice of less-than-effective leaders, and this may be more true within the framework of the church. Elderships everywhere struggle with this and it causes discontent, poor performance, and disorganization. Because elders have listened to the input and assessed the legitimate needs of the congregation, they will be more able to choose good people to accomplish various tasks within the work of the church, and then step back and allow them to do their work.

I am thinking of a man who had assumed the role of director of a week of Christian encampment and quickly began to feel the burden of the task. Desiring to establish quickly an atmosphere of control and authority, he announced during the first assembly that nothing would be done without his approval and management. Big mistake! He soon learned that there were decisions to be made and tasks to be done that he was not equipped or trained to accomplish. He had a great staff working with him and he quickly learned that it was time for him to step back, let them do what they do, and embrace his role as encampment director.[27]

In addition to the first suggestion of being aware of the presence and function of others within the organization (church), the second suggests that the humble servant leader will be aware of his needs, personal development, and attitude. One example of this is that such a leader must spend time in self-reflection where time is spent in prayer, reflection, and contemplation of himself and his task. Gayle Beebe wrote that "one of the greatest challenges facing a new leader is developing the capacity for moral self-reflection. So often what distinguishes great leaders from also-rans is whether or not we can develop a capacity to self-correct. Leaders get off track. We overreact. We walk into situations and do not respond as we should."[28]

It is a well-known fact, but one that is too often overlooked or even ignored by leaders everywhere: there is always room for improvement. Perhaps the apostle Paul had this in mind, at least in part, when he wrote, "Not that I have already obtained this or am already perfect, but I press on to make it my own, because Christ Jesus has made me his own. Brothers, I do not consider that I have made it my own. But thing I do: forgetting what lies ahead, I press on toward the goal for the prize of the upward call of God in Christ Jesus (Phil. 3.12–14)." When leaders (elders) recognize and embrace where they are in life, realizing what has been accomplished and what still remains undone, they can then plot their future course, improve upon it and become more effective shepherds, guides, mentors, and teachers.

---

[27] Some of you who know me might remember that I am the one who made this mistake as I assumed the role of director of Junior Week so many, many years ago. It was indeed a humbling and learning experience.

[28] Gayle, Beebe, *An Effective Leader*, 30.

Leaders who are aware of themselves—their strengths and weaknesses, their liabilities, their personal resources—have spent time in self-evaluation and self-reflection. This can be accomplished through a variety of means: keeping a journal, and receiving feedback and input from others regarding that leader's performance, among others. It is too often unknown, forgotten, or ignored that the pastoral work of elders and preachers, for example, are not only within their congregations, but within themselves. Leaders must take the time for self-evaluation and self-renewal or their leadership will suffer.

The literature of ministry and leadership reflects this need through the plethora of books on the subject. Hundreds, even thousands, of books are available that address the need for self-reflection and personal development. Here is a brief sampling (see bibliography for references):

- In their two volumes on congregational leadership, Norman Shawchuck and Roger Heuser (*Managing the Congregation: Building Effective Systems to Serve People* and *Leading the Congregation: Caring for Yourself While Serving the People*) observed the "interior attitudes of the leader," "the leader's spirituality," and the leader as "a person before God."
- In *The Shaping of an Effective Leader: Eight Formative Principles of Leadership*, Gayle Beebe included the concerns of character, competence, convictions, and legacy.
- Ruth Barton wrote of leaders losing the soul of their work, being aware of what lies beneath the leader, one's spiritual conversion, spiritual calling, the leader's spiritual journey, "spiritual rhythms" in leaders, and loneliness, isolation, and community in her book, *Strengthening the Soul of Your Leadership: Seeking God in the Crucible of Ministry*.

- Coming from the other direction, John Maxwell, in *Developing the Leaders Around You: How to Help Others Reach Their Full Potential*, wrote of leaders being the mentors, equippers, and nurturers of leaders developing and growing in their task.

These and so many other books, as well as thousands of articles in periodicals, journals, and blogs, remind leaders to take care of themselves personally, spiritual, and emotionally. A leader who is overwrought, overworked, overwhelmed, and underappreciated cannot be as effective as possible.

The humble servant leader will also be wise to admit his mistakes, learn from them, and move on. Jeanie Prime and Elizabeth Salib associate a leader's mistake with teachable moments:

> When leaders showcase their own personal growth, they legitimize the growth and learning of others; by admitting to their own imperfections, they make it okay for others to be fallible, too. We tend to connect with people who share their imperfections and foibles—they appear more 'human,' more like us. Particularly in diverse workgroups, displays of humility may help to remind group members of their common humanity and shared objectives.[29]

Mistakes are the footprints of good leaders, for when one stops to look back at past attempts and failures, he sees the path taken to effective and successful results. "Unless I try, I cannot succeed" is something I heard years ago. I do not remember who said it or how came to hear it, but its message rings so true in my mind. No one ever failed by not trying; but no one ever succeeded either. Servant leaders who demonstrate humility in their task are not afraid to admit their mistakes. Those mistakes are indicative of trial and error, victory and defeat, failure and success, and all of

---

[29] Prime and Salib, "Humble Leaders," 2.

it adds to the image of a leader who is a humble servant at heart.

As the leader is willing to admit his mistakes, he must also be willing to accept and embrace ambiguity and uncertainty. As a symptom of a lack of humility, some leaders find it difficult to admit that they do not know the answer, the right direction, and the next move. No one—anyone—has all of the answers and no one, except our Lord Jesus Christ, has been or will be omniscient or omnipotent. Accepting that truth allows the humble servant leader to realize that leadership sometimes, but not always, is being the one willing to be the first down that path, or the first to open that door, or the first to take the leap. While good leaders will always gather as much information as possible, sometimes the necessary information is not available by a certain deadline, so decisions must be made and action must be taken.

I know of a man in a Midwestern state who is, to this writer, the epitome of the humble manager and leader. In his work he is called upon to build, tear down, and repair on a regular basis. When a specific mechanical task would lie ahead of him, he would say, "Let's open it up and see what we get into." In other words, it is time to open it up, assess what is wrong, see what can be done, and what is needed to fix it. Many times, when I would ask how the repair went, he would reply that the effort was unsuccessful because they did not have the necessary tool(s), they did not have enough time (there was much more to do than was initially thought), or he realized he did not have, at that time, enough knowledge of what needed to be done…yet. Days would pass and when asked again, he would smile and report that the task was successfully completed.

Humility is a key element of servant leadership, including the willingness to embrace uncertainty and mistakes. As the leader is a servant to his followers and the organization, such as the elders must be servants of the congregation they shepherd, as well as the Lord, leaders are also servants to their task and that will always involve mistakes and uncertainty.

Ethics

A second foundational, essential trait that emerges for me is ethics. It should be obvious that being humble servants demands that leaders are ethical as well: ethical in attitude and purpose, seeking to do what is best, what is good for all and not just for themselves. Beebe wrote that "the secret of success in life and business" all comes down to ethics.[30] Are ethics a part of effective servant leadership, however? Northouse believed so. He associated servant leadership with ethical leadership, which carries a strong sense of respect, service, justice, honesty, and community.[31] Northouse may have a legitimate point; perhaps not. The connection of servant leadership with ethical leadership is intriguing, for respect, service, honesty, and community seem to coincide with both. But, what is ethical leadership and is there a true connection with servant leadership?

Ethical leadership focuses on leading through the acquiring of knowledge and the desire to do what is right. In essence, ethical leadership can be divided into two parts: (1) the need to act and make decisions ethically; (2) the need to be ethical in attitude and interactions with others; that is with those that he or she leads. Ethical leaders stress a high degree of integrity that promotes a sense of trustworthiness, which is essential to the leader-follower dynamic. Leading ethically, then, is about the display of character and integrity where a leader's ethical beliefs, values, and decisions enhance the process of decision making.

I am thinking of a famous and popular media-oriented preach-

---

[30] Beebe, *An Effective Leader*, 26.

[31] Northouse, Leadership, 384–385.

er who enjoys much success and prosperity. His preaching is, in my opinion, very shallow and his time before his audience is spent largely basking in the adulation and praise of his followers, which he appears to covet. He continually and consistently reminds his audience of *his* work, *his* ministry, *his* facility, and *his* successes. While the Lord is mentioned, the emphasis, at least in my mind, is focused on himself as he encourages them to follow him, be like him, and continue to contribute to his success.

So what does it mean to be "ethical"? A dictionary defines it as "relating to morals; morally correct; honorable."[32] So then, ethics and the task of being ethical focus on the desire for morality, moral behavior, and the demonstration of what is considered correct and honorable. This is far too general for our purposes, for as I will address later, what is correct and honorable is often subject to debate: what is moral, correct, and honorable for one is not so for another. To simply label leadership as "ethical" is indecisive and undetermined.

Ethics and character are also closely related. Beebe placed one's character as a foundation of effective leadership.[33] She added that "Character is built on our understanding of ethics."[34] Ethics are the codes or principles on which one's character depends. Ethics develop at an early age and can be instrumental to building character. Howell wrote, "Character can be defined as a person's moral constitution, in which is embedded a stable set of values."[35]

In this way, character is something developed through the desire and need for an ethical foundation. While one might understand and even accept that secular leaders may not seek high

---

[32] *Oxford Illustrated American Dictionary* (London, New York, Sydney, Moscow: DK Publishing, Inc., 1998), 276.

[33] Beebe, *An Effective Leader*, 25.

[34] Ibid., 26.

[35] Howell, *Servants*, 296.

levels of character and ethics, it is essential that congregational leaders—elders—will make such a priority. In fact, not only is it essential, but it is also a biblical commandment; Paul, in this list of characteristics (qualifications) of elders, demanded that they be above reproach (1 Tim. 3.2). In fact, it is the first of these characteristics or qualifications. Did the apostle cite this first by way of emphasis over the others? Perhaps, for he will make a similar point in verse seven. Actually, how one is perceived by others is a significant concern in this first epistle to Timothy (cf. 2.2, 10; 5.7, 14; 6.1). For Paul, good and moral character is essential.

Integrity is also a component of ethical character. Integrity can be defined as "moral uprightness; honesty; wholeness; soundness."[36] James Kouzes and Barry Posner, in a survey of almost 1,500 managers within the United States, asked the question, "What values…do you look for and admire in your superiors?" Out of over 250 various values given, the ethical characteristic of integrity—defined as being truthful, trustworthy, having character, and having convictions—was number one.[37] In a similar study, McCormick Theological Seminary conducted "a large nationwide study" in 1989–90 of the various roles and characteristics congregational leaders must embrace.[38] The "Better Preparation for Ministry Project" used focus groups to gather and assimilate information based upon a ranked order, the first of which was personal integrity.

---

[36] *Oxford Illustrated Dictionary*, 422.

[37] James M. Kouzes and Barry Z. Posner, *The Leadership Challenge: How to Get Extraordinary Things Done in Organizations* (San Francisco: Jossey-Bass Publishers, 1987), 267.

[38] Shawchuck and Heuser, *Leading the Congregation*, 115. The survey was focused on the expectations of congregations and "judiciary executives" regarding the role of the congregational pastor as is practiced within general denominational Christianity. However, the implications of the study and its conclusions clearly impact the role of congregational elders as pastors and shepherds that is the focus of this book.

Integrity is often associated in a way with the exercise of power and authority, where moral character must be considered essential. Biblically, this can be clearly seen in the divine instructions regarding the task of stewardship. Rendered from the Greek *oikonomos* as "steward or manager," the task is associated biblically with those who had been given power and authority over a household. "The steward-as-manager owned nothing," wrote Shawchuck and Heuser, "but his reputation was made with the ability to manage with integrity, or at least with prudence."[39]

Paul wrote, "Moreover, it is required of stewards that they be found trustworthy" (1 Cor. 4.2). Such trustworthiness, such integrity, is a foundational element of being stewards, for the steward is entrusted with what is not his own, but what has been placed into his care so that those resources will be used properly and most effectively. In the Parable of the Dishonest Steward (or Manager), "a certain rich man who had a manager" heard accusations against his steward for "wasting his [the rich man's] possessions." The rich man called his steward to him and said, "What is this I hear about you? Turn in the account of your management, for you can no longer be manager" (Luke 16.1–2). Add to this Paul's admonition concerning the characteristics (qualifications) of elders, insisting that the elder "must manage his own household well, with all dignity keeping his children submissive, for if someone does not know how to manage his own household, how will he care for God's church?" (1 Tim. 3.4–5).

The biblical steward is a fine example of integrity, for congregational leaders must realize and embrace that what they shepherd does not belong to them, but to the Lord; they are the caretakers of it (cf. Titus 1.7). They are entrusted with such precious and divine things, eternal in scope, and they must carry out their stewardship with integrity. Many modern-day ministry and con-

---

[39] Shawchuck and Heuser, *Managing the Congregation*, 21.

gregational leaders will do well to remember their own stewardship, including this author. We do not offer things in our service to the Lord that belong to us; we are in control of nothing except our obedience to be the shepherds, teachers, preachers, and examples the Lord commands us to be.

Paul used the concept of stewardship to describe the obligations of his ministry. In his first letter to the church of Corinth, the apostle wrote, "For if I preach the gospel, that gives me no ground for boasting. For necessity is laid upon me. Woe to me if I do not preach the gospel! For if I do this of my own will, I have a reward, but if not of my own will, I am still entrusted with a stewardship" (1 Cor. 9.16–17). He told the church in Colosse that he had become a minister "according to the stewardship from God that was given to me for you, to make the word of God fully known" (Col. 1.25).

So then, the work of ethical leaders is one of integrity and moral character. Their work must be focused on the people being led and the leader must be keenly aware of how his decisions will impact others. In this way, ethical leadership seeks to serve the greater good rather than focusing on what is self-serving. Motivating followers to put the needs or interests of the group ahead of their own is another quality of ethical leaders. Motivating involves engaging others in an intellectual and emotional commitment between leaders and followers that makes both parties equally responsible in the pursuit of a common goal.

A problem with the dynamic known as "ethical leadership" is that it is based on doing what is "right" and that, as I pointed out earlier regarding what is moral and honorable, is difficult to define. The world varies in its view of what is right and what is not right: individuality, cultural differences, religious variations all impact the idea of "right" in different ways. Numerous examples abound. For example, cultural differences impact the way people feel about race relations, gender discussions, and economic issues. The ideologies of the broad worldview of "religion" drive considerations such as orthodoxy, doctrine, and truth, among others. These considerations are founded, in part, on the varieties of sacred writ that describe the spiritual and practical elements of how a religion is observed.

Of course, congregational servant leaders must be ethical and an understanding of ethics must be founded upon Scripture. Howell wrote, "For the biblical leader [stable values] are conditioned by revealed truth recorded only in Holy Scripture."[40] Howell noticed the apostle Paul as an example of this in 1 Tim. 3.1–13 and Titus 1.5–9 as he established "a set of criteria for elders and deacons that centers around moral virtues that spring from and evidence godly character…Paul's philosophy of leadership is character-grounded rather than geared around personality, role, temperament, or gifting. This is because character possesses the staying power and impact potential necessary for a lasting legacy. Timothy and Titus will succeed in their pastoral ministries to the degree that they give careful attention to growing in godliness and setting an example for the believers in faith (Godward), love (manward), and integrity (selfward) (1 Tim. 4.7–8, 12, 16; Tit. 2.7–8, 15; 3.8). These three areas intersect in the character of the godly leader."[41]

Ethical leadership is centered on a definition and expectation far different from a secular view where what is moral, right, correct, and honorable depends on the cultural, situational, intentional, and directional arenas in which such leadership is done. Ethical leadership in congregational servant leadership is theocentric (God-centered) and operates from a biblical modus operandi, as should all leadership, actually.

---

[40] Howell, *Servant*, 296.

[41] Ibid.

Communication and Listening

A third and final foundational, essential trait that emerges for me is the art of listening, truly hearing what others are saying. A consideration of listening, of course, is part of the larger concern of communication, for listening is a form of communication and a means by which communication is done. While tempting, to be sure, I will not focus on the dynamics of communication in leadership, which is of major concern and consideration within the larger study of leadership dynamics. My focus is that part of communication that is engaged in listening and so then informs the task of servant leadership.

Alexander Strauch, quoting Bruce Stabbert, wrote, "One of the most essential ingredients of any kind of teamwork is good communications."[42] Communication is the process of verbal and nonverbal interchange of words, gestures, and body language, as well as the imparting of information. It should be understood and accepted that the communication of information is essential to any task, especially within the field of leadership. That includes, of course, the leadership of a congregation. Without information, one cannot know what needs to be known.

Recall the example I offered earlier of the preacher who felt he had pertinent information regarding the congregation in which he served, and his desire for he and elders to meet so he could share that information with them. Recall also that the elder who related the story to me quickly informed him that he, the preacher, did not decide when a meeting would take place or what information would be shared. Such decisions and actions were for the elders and the elders only. That incident is sad not only because of the

---

[42] Alexander Strauch, *Meetings That Work: A Guide to Effective Elder's Meetings*. (Colorado Springs, CO: Lewis and Roth Publishers, 2001), 33; Bruce Stabbert, *The Team Concept: Paul's Church Leadership Pattern or Ours?* (Tacoma, WA: Hegg, 1982), 177–81.

non-servant-like attitude of that elder, but also because of the loss of potentially effective and vital information for the growth and development of that congregation. That preacher, trained and experienced in ministry, perhaps had something to offer that would have been essential to the growth of that congregation spiritually and numerically. It is essential that leaders are engaged in the act and art of effective communication; receiving information and ideas that may be pivotal to their work, as well as the task of those who serve under, and for the organization they serve.

As I mentioned just above, communication is done through verbal (words) and nonverbal means (gestures; body language). Let us briefly examine those individually. Verbal communication is the more recognized and understood, of course, for we readily identify such in our conversations, speeches, lectures, and other forms of communication where information is given through the speaking or writing of words.[43] In the secular world, we see this done through educational and informative television, through the written and spoken news media as well as social media, and through the printed pages of newspapers, magazines, periodicals, and journals. All of these means are staples of our reception and delivery of information.

Nonverbal communication is also well-known, but perhaps less so than its verbal counterpart. Nonverbal communication is done without the expression of words, verbally and/or on the printed page. Nonverbal communication is done through gestures and body language. Examples of communicating through gestures would include the pointing of a finger or holding up the palm of the hand. Examples of communicating through body language would include the way one sits in a chair, the physical body angle one takes in respect to the participant(s) in the conversation, the

---

[43] Communication dynamics often separates verbal and written communication, but I am including both under the category of verbal communication.

rolling of the eyes, or shaking or nodding the head, and the lack or the intensity of eye contact.

Leaders must come to recognize and accept the existence and function of verbal and nonverbal communication if they will lead effectively through the gathering of information. It is recognizing the verbal communication of innuendo or insinuation (the real meaning lies behind what is said: "Why can we not make a decision unless Tom is here?"), or the use of generalities ("We can never seem to get anything worthwhile done around here!"). It is recognizing the nonverbal signals of someone who refuses to look toward the speaker, the suddenly waving off of the hand, or slouching in the chair.

Consider this scenario. The elders of the Main Street congregation have called a meeting for the elders, deacons, and preacher(s) on a particular night. The night arrives and the conference room is filled with all who are expected to be involved, except one of the deacons, the one who missed the last elder-deacons-preacher(s) meeting two months prior, and the one who has been talking down some of the decisions and plans to other members of the congregation. The elders must see such behavior, such verbal and nonverbal communication as a bright warning sign of potential conflict. The meeting starts with a prayer and the elders begin to articulate concerns, plans, and ideas they wish to discuss with all in attendance, to then present a plan of action later to the congregation. It must be noticed that one of the six elders remains quiet and somewhat disconnected, even distracted. Why? Is he distracted by something outside of the meeting, or is his distraction emerging from a concern he has with the contents of the meeting? It should also be noticed that six of the seventeen deacons, who are sitting together at the far end of the conference table, express several nonverbal signals (looking down or away, rolling the eyes, doodling on a notepad, etc.) when one of the elders and two of their fellow deacons speaks. Finally, two the deacons repeat generalities such as "We never..." or "We always...," and seemingly disagree with every suggestion or idea presented. No one is against everything, but they seem to be just that.

It is imperative that the elders, as well as the deacons and preacher(s), recognize and embrace the existence of such negative, but informative, communication. It is essential that all recognize and embrace the need for good communication whenever they meet, and good communication when they present information, ideas, and plans to the congregation.

All this concerns the act and art of listening, for good communication is, in part, about good listening. Greenleaf wrote:

> Listening, as I use it here, is not just keeping still, or even remembering what is said. Listening is an attitude, an attitude toward other people and what they are trying to express. It begins with a genuine interest that is manifest in close attention, and it goes on to understanding in depth—whence cometh wisdom. It is openness to communication—openness within the widest possible frame of reference—openness to hear the prophetic voices that are trying to speak to us all of the time.[44]

Notice two pertinent points made by Greenleaf: (1) listening is an attitude, and (2) from listening comes understanding, even wisdom. That is so true, for through listening one can hear what is *really* going on, what are the *real* concerns and obstacles, as well as what others are *really* saying, implying, and feeling.

Maxwell listed several values found in effective and careful listening.[45] His list emerges from the reality of a very negative

---

[44] Greenleaf, *Servant Leadership*, 313.

[45] John C. Maxwell, *Becoming a Person of Influence: How to Positively Impact the Lives of Others* (Nashville, Atlanta, London, Vancouver: Thomas Nelson Publishers, 1997), 81–84.

practice when two or more people engage in conversation: listening only to prepare for a response.

- Listening shows respect
- Listening builds relationships
- Listening increases knowledge
- Listening generates ideas
- Listening builds loyalty
- Listening is a great way to help others and yourself

I am not going to take the time to unpack each of these values—you are capable of doing that yourself and can do so based on your own experiences, knowledge, and perspectives. So then, read this list of values again and contemplate how each of them might inform the task of listening, as well as the task of effective leadership. You might ask questions, such as:

- How does listening show respect or generate ideas?
- What are ways I have seen knowledge increased through effective listening?
- How might I learn to listen more effectively?

Maxwell offered the statement (not his own), "No man would listen to you talk if he didn't know it was his turn next."[46] He commented, "Unfortunately, that accurately describes the way too many people approach communication—they're too busy waiting for their turn to really listen to others. But people of influence understand the incredible value of becoming a good listener."[47] I recall many, many years ago when I was attempting to have a Bible study with a friend and co-worker who hailed from a particular denomination. Our theological and practical differences had led to much discussion, little of which was very productive.

---

[46] Ibid., 80.
[47] Ibid.

The problem—I was equally guilty—was a lack of desire to truly listen to one another. We spent too much time anticipating our turn to speak, contemplating in our minds how to frame the next eloquent response that would bring the other to a swift defeat. While I would not have accepted his understanding of certain theological and practical values, nor would he have done, we failed to have any effective, reasonable discussion because neither one of us truly listened to the other.

Leaders must realize the benefits of listening, really listening, to what is being said. This implies paying attention to what is important, what needs to be understood and accepted, as well what is *not* being said. Consider Jesus' instruction in Rev. 3.20: "Behold, I stand at the door and knock. If anyone hears my voice and opens the door, I will come in to him and eat with him, and he with me." Leaders must pray that Jesus will knock, and that they will hear, and the *door* will be opened to them and their task. Shawchuck and Heuser commented, "Christ is always standing at our door, always knocking. But unless those inside the house are quiet and listening they will not hear the knocking, for Christ never knocks very loudly—just persistently."[48] I am not sure that Jesus never knocks loudly—sometimes He might need to pound on the door to get us to listen, perhaps—but I agree that He does so persistently.

Some of us will remember the "Citizens Band Radio" (CB Radio) craze that emerged a few decades ago out of the communication system used by the trucking industry, and was adopted by the general public. Several catch-phrases became popular within it, including, "Got your ears on?" The query implied a call for attention, to listen to what was about to be said. Jesus repeatedly instructed the seven churches of Asia Minor, "He who has an ear, let him hear what the Spirit says to the churches" (Rev. 2.7, 11, 17,

---

[48] Shawchuck and Heuser, *Managing the Congregation*, 127.

29; 3.6, 13, 22). Notice the call to attention, "He who has an ear, let him hear...," for it implies more than just hearing words. It is a command to effectively listen to the words of the Spirit.

Effective listening, then, comes within the silence of paying attention: not speaking, but truly hearing what is being said. Stillness and silence is a biblical concept. "Be still before the Lord," wrote the psalmist, "and wait patiently for him" (Ps. 37.7). Shawchuck and Heuser wrote, "This interior stillness is more than being still and letting your mind wander into various dusty closets of its choosing. Rather, it is a purposeful stillness—and an openness to metanoia.[49] Just as the Queen's guard stands still—and yet fully attentive to hear Her Majesty's distant footfall—so the silence we suggest is an active listening in stillness."[50]

Such stillness, and silence as well, removes some of the barriers to effective listening because the implication is not merely stillness and silence of voice (not talking), but of the mind as well. It is an ultimate form of paying attention. The psalmist recorded the command of God, "Be still, and know that I am God" (Ps. 46.10). It can be argued that speaking when it is unnecessary, even detrimental, is a form of arrogance, but stillness and silence is a form of humility. The former can be seen in people who must always have the last word or, as the saying goes, enjoy hearing the sound of their own voice. The latter is an ideal of any leader. Bill[51] had a problem with speaking when he should have been still and silent, listening respectfully and intently. As an elder, he was faced with numerous issues, conflicts, needs, and decisions, but he rarely stopped to listen to others. On one occasion, he was asked to sit with an individual who was undergoing a spiritual crisis in

---

[49] *Metanoia* is a Greek word implying repentance, a change of heart, a turning away from something, or a change of (moral) direction.

[50] Shawchuck and Heuser, *Managing the Congregation*, 128.

[51] Not his real name.

her life. The young woman began to express her concerns, but within a very few minutes she was interrupted and the elder began to speak, telling her how she should feel, what she should do, and that her conflict was not really that serious. Later, both of them approached me. The elder expressed how she was fortunate to have come to him, while she felt even in greater crisis, lamenting that he had not even listened to her, but did most of the talking.

Servant leaders listen, and they do so respectfully, attentively, and humbly. Listening allows the servant leader to know, to discern, to decide, and to act. Shawchuck and Heuser commented, "The leaders simply learn to listen in order to discover what is bubbling up throughout the congregation. As you move about among the members of the congregation and the participants in the congregation's program, listen. Listen for new ministry and program ideas. Make note of who makes which suggestions. When you hear the same idea three times, gather those persons together and get them talking about their idea. You will soon know whether this is an idea whose time has come by the quality of their discussions and their degree of commitment to their own idea."[52]

---

[52] Shawchuck and Heuser, *Leading the Congregation*, 172.

TWO | The Biblical Model of Servant Leadership

One major issue in leadership studies is the introduction of an effective model of practice: what does and what does not work. Are all leadership models the same (e.g. transformational, authentic, team, or transactional leadership) or does one rise above the others? Within the myriad theories (e.g. contingency and leader-member exchange theory) and approaches (e.g. trait, skills, style, and situational approach) is one better than another? Does it really matter what type or theory of leadership is adopted just as long as some sort of leadership is practiced? That depends on what and who is being led, and who is doing the leading.

In chapter one, I examined organizational leadership overall and included an assessment of servant leadership and some key concerns, both secular and spiritual. This book, however, is about spiritual, congregational leadership, that which exists and functions within the place where worship, spiritual fellowship, and works of ministry are done through the efforts of those who comprise its population. As was indicated in the first chapter, the church can be studied as an organization with most of the concerns of an organization. I must emphasize, however, that to leave it at that, the church as an organization, leaves the task unfinished. The church is spiritual and so bigger than anything secular, and so in that way it must also be understood and appreciated.

I will emphasize servant leadership as an effective model of congregational leadership rather than leadership within corporate, political, educational, and military organizations.[1] This book proposes that servant leadership, as it is understood in the field of leadership research, is capable of standing on its own. While there are some gaps and weaknesses in the model as it has been developed and implemented, I believe that the philosophy and intentionality of servant leadership as a foundational platform of practice is of substantial importance to the task of congregational leadership, as well as followership, a concept I will discuss later.

Jeffrey Jones wrote, "Despite its secular origins and focus, Greenleaf's concept of the servant leader resonates well with biblical teaching."[2] Servant leadership is a legitimate model of congregational leadership and the Bible contains information and applications of it that help to realize the potential of this model of leadership. Consider Malphurs:

> A biblical image that is most common and dominant for leaders is that of a servant. And this is the image I use in my definition of Christian leaders: Christian leaders are servants with credibility and capabilities, who are able to influence people with a particular context to pursue their God-given direction. Many leaders in both Testaments are called or refer to themselves as servants. The following are some noteworthy examples: Abra-

---

[1] It is understood in this book that a congregation is, by function, an organization. I will discuss this in greater detail in chapter seven. It is also understood that while the servant leadership model is perhaps best suited for spiritual, church leadership, it can also be effective to some extent within most or any other organizations.

[2] Jeffery D. Jones, *Heart, Mind, and Strength: Theory and Practice for Congregational Leadership* (Herndon, VA: The Alban Institute, 2008), 12.

ham, Joseph, Moses, Joshua, Nehemiah, David, Daniel, Christ, Paul, and Peter.[3]

In Drury's mind:

> Servant leadership theory can hardly be rejected by a Church built on the life, death, and resurrection of Jesus Christ. Jesus Christ was the ultimate example of servanthood, by leaving all the glory of heaven to come as a human and accepting the way of the cross. His earthly ministry built up a Church that spread the gospel to the ends of the earth after He ascended into heaven again.[4]

One can agree with Drury's assessment, for the concepts of servanthood and servant leadership should fit nicely within the place and function of any congregation.

The Apostle Paul and Acts 20

Consider the apostle Paul's admonishment of the elders of the church in Ephesus in Acts 20. Read with me verses 28–32:

> Pay careful attention to yourselves and to all the flock, in which the Holy Spirit has made you overseers, to care for the church of God, which he obtained with his own blood. I know that after my departure fierce wolves will come in among you, not sparing the flock; and from among your own selves will arise men speaking twisted things, to draw away the disciples after them. Therefore be alert, remembering that for three years I did not cease night or day to admonish every one with tears. And now I commend you to God and to the word of his grace, which is able to build you up and to give you the inheritance among all those who are sanctified.

Paul's emphasis on the role of the elders as guards, protectors, and guides is clear. He reminded them that their task was

---
[3] Malphurs, *Being leaders*, 33.

[4] Drury, *Handbook*, 22.

centered on the needs of the congregation in Ephesus; it was not about their position as leaders (too often egotistical in nature), but their task as servants who would be the leaders of the congregation.

First: Pay Attention. I have noticed several significant elements of Paul's words to the elders of the church in Ephesus that make significant connections to effective leaders in the church. First, they were to "pay attention" to themselves and to the congregation. Not exclusive to only servant leadership, but part of leadership dynamics in general, leaders must be aware of their own situations, as well as the situations of their followers. Self-care among leaders is vital to their ability to effectively carry out their task. This element of leadership has been emphasized for quite some time, and is not isolated to servant leadership but is a component of leadership on a number of levels and in a variety of settings. It is, however, of primary concern within the servant leader model.

There is much to be commended within Howell's book, *Servants of the Servant: A Biblical Theology of Leadership* (2003). I will cite him several times through the remainder of this book because of his insights and perspectives of the servant leader model. I must challenge, however, Howell's insistence that, "But God does not depend upon heroes, he uses smudged and unattractive 'jars of clay' (2 Cor. 4.7)."[5] To be fair, Howell referred to "the most idealized portrait found in romantic novels about super heroes," so his point is well taken: the Bible is not about a collection of super heroes, but those jars of clay that carried out the divine tasks given to them. The Bible is, however, full of heroes, people who were simple jars of clay that finished the jobs with which they were entrusted. They were fishermen, priests, tax collectors, kings, queens, widows, farmers, and animal herders; they were also God's people accomplishing God's work.

---

[5] Howell, *Servants of the Servant*, 296.

Paul's counsel to the elders of the Ephesian church to "pay careful attention" to themselves is significant because that is something a jar of clay who is tasked with the work of God must do. According to the Athenian philosopher Socrates (469–399 BC), "The unexamined life is not worth living."[6] Paul's challenge for the elders in Ephesus to pay careful attention to themselves is the challenge of self-examination. Shawchuck and Heuser list the task of self-examination as the fourth of four qualities of religious leadership and warn the reader, "One of the greatest dangers stalking all religious leaders is that of becoming so busy or so bored, so proud or so depressed, that the things they desire most, as well as their actions, go unexamined."[7] Self-awareness, according to Northouse, is a key component of authentic leadership, which he defines as "the personal insights of the leader" such as strengths and weaknesses, as well as one's impact upon others.[8]

Such self-examination and self-awareness take courage because they can show a less-than-attractive reflection of oneself. The task is essential, however, for how else will a leader know his past and present, and so then his future? Without such self-examination, paying attention to oneself, a leader will not be able to separate the grain from the chaff, the good from the bad, and the effective from the ineffective. I propose that this was part of the change of heart and attitude of the younger son in the Parable of the Prodigal Son, sometimes referred to as the Parable of the Two Sons (Luke 15.11–32). After a period of reckless living that led to a time of tremendous need that became so bad he would have fought the pigs for their food, "he came to himself" and took stock of his present situation compared to his past, making the

---

[6] Plato, "Dialogues," *Apology*, 38a.

[7] Norman Shawchuck and Roger Heuser, *Leading the Congregation: Caring for Yourself While Serving the People* (Nashville: Abingdon Press, 1993), 36.

[8] Northouse, *Leadership*, 207, 217.

decision to return home to live as a servant to his father; of course his father refused and honored him in his return home. His self-examination, while disheartening, allowed him to become the man and perhaps leader he should have been. It is important that a leader pay attention to himself.

Howell offered three "trajectories that penetrate the fundamental identity of all servant leaders:" (1) character, or who the leader is and is becoming; (2) motive, or why the leader undertakes a course of action; and (3) agenda, or what the leader pursues as the defined mission."[9] Howell concluded the point by insisting that these trajectories are "the core constituents and interrelated foci of the kind of leadership enjoined in the Holy Scripture."[10] These questions of who, why, and what are essential in leaders paying attention to themselves as Paul advised.

What is the "who" or "character" of effective leadership? One day, long ago, Moses was tending the flock of his father-in-law Jethro near Horeb, the mountain of God (Ex. 3.1). He approached a bush nearby that was set ablaze, but was not consumed in the flames. Upon reaching the vicinity of this very unusual sight, Moses heard the voice of God and was afraid. God told Moses that he had heard the affliction of his people enslaved in Egypt and said, "Come, I will send you to Pharaoh that you may bring my people, the children of Israel, out of Egypt" (Ex 3.10).

Imagine Moses' thoughts, concerns, misgivings, apprehensions, mistakes, victories, and fears as he carried out the task God had given him. Imagine also the times of self-appraisal that accompanied the myriad emotions Moses faced. Consider the tent of meeting that was erected outside the camp, "And everyone who sought the Lord would go out to the tent of meeting" (Ex. 33.7). Moses certainly went out of the tent and "Thus the Lord used to

---

[9] Ibid.

[10] Ibid.

speak to Moses face to face, as a man speaks to his friend" (11). It is granted that Moses used those times in the presence of God to express his concerns and seek advice, but consider also that this may have been a time for Moses to assess himself and his work for God; to "pay careful attention" to himself as he answered the questions of who, why, and what.

Paul addressed the character of a leader to Timothy in 1 Timothy 3.1–7, the so-called "qualifications" of elders. In this passage Paul insisted that elders are to be "above reproach," "sober-minded, self-controlled, respectable, hospitable," and "well thought of by outsiders." For Paul, such characteristics are essential to elders as leaders.

What is the "why" or "motive" of an effective leader? Consider Nehemiah as an example of the "why" (motive) of an effective leader. When he learned of the deplorable condition of Jerusalem, the city of his fathers, he asked permission from the king, Artaxerxes, to go to the city and repair it (Neh. 2.3–8). After his arrival and inspection of the city, Nehemiah then approached the people and told them of his intentions: "Come, let us build the wall of Jerusalem, that we may no longer suffer derision. And I told them of the hand of my God that had been upon me for good" (17a). When he was opposed by Sanballat, Tobiah, and Geshem, Nehemiah proclaimed, "The God of heaven will makes us prosper, and we his servants will arise and build" (20a). An effective spiritual leader will always center his motives upon the will and power of God.

Nehemiah's example of proper motives (the "why" of leadership), and that of so many more,[11] emerged from a desire for the welfare of those involved, as well as a concern for obedience to the commandments of God. This is a concern of paying attention to

---

[11] Other examples would include Joseph and his leadership in Egypt (cf. Gen. 41), David

oneself, a self-appraisal of one's motives for action. Howell refers to this as a "doxological motive" where "a passion for God's honor" is a driving force behind what a leader does.[12]

Finally, what is the "how" or "agenda" of an effective leader? Howell wrote:

> Servant-leaders are not visionaries who devise a brilliant plan, then by dint of personal charisma draw others to fulfill those ambitions. Rather they are faithful stewards of the divine mandate—to fish and to feed, to evangelize and to teach, to pioneer and to pastor. Biblical leadership maintains a laser-like concentration on God's clearly stated agenda, that is, the evangelization of the lost, the edification of the saved, and the establishment of vital churches.[13]

A central component of a servant leader's agenda is that his task is *theocentric*, what is centered upon God. Effective leadership, spiritual or secular, is not leader-focused, for to be so, all that is done would be to enhance and develop the leader himself. Sadly, this has been the norm in the past and that erroneous path is not isolated to the secular world alone, but all too often is found, even in a supposedly more educated society, in the religious world. Far too many church leaders within the broader ecclesiastical world seek to remain the central figures advocating their agendas, their churches, their results, their visions, and their own places in the spotlight.

Howell continued, "Servant leaders take the initiative to bring others to a passionate commitment to what is on the heart of God, the extension of his saving rule over individuals and communities both qualitatively (holiness of character) and quantitatively

---

[12] Howell, *Servants of the Servant*, 299.
[13] Ibid., 301.

(expansion of the unreached frontiers)."[14] Spiritual leaders do not create their own unique agendas, but carry out a divine task; their agendas are in regard to that task. Paul repeatedly emphasized that church leaders care for the church of God (Acts 20.28; 1 Tim. 3.5). To Titus, Paul wrote that the church leader is God's steward (Titus 1.7). Peter encouraged church leaders to "shepherd the flock of God that is among you...as God would have you" (1 Peter 5.2, 3). Effective servant leaders will extend the divine mission of the church to the congregation. The agenda belongs to God; the mission belongs to God; the church belongs to God; the work belongs to God.

Second: The Holy Spirit. A second element of Paul's challenge to the elders in Ephesus was that their function as overseers of the congregation was by the design of the Holy Spirit. It goes without saying the Holy Spirit is a significant and pivotal force and presence within the biblical text. The Spirit teaches (Luke 12.12), the Spirit pours God's love into our hearts (Rom. 5.5), and it helps us in our weaknesses and intercedes in our prayers (Rom. 8.26). The Holy Spirit helps us in our spiritual walk so we can bear the fruit of the Spirit (Gal. 5.14–26). So then we are strengthened by the Spirit (Eph. 3.16) and armored with the sword of the Spirit (Eph. 6.17). The Holy Spirit bears witness to us [through the word of God] (Heb. 10.15–17) and testifies the truth to us (1 John 5.6b). As Shawchuck and Heuser wrote:

> The life of the Spirit within the congregation needs tending, other-wise it will not bear the fruit and ministries of the Spirit. It is perhaps especially important for liberal social activists and conservative evangelicals to hear that what the church lacks today is not work, activity, projects, or a commitment to save the lost or the suffering. What is missing, or at least very scarce, are the elements of prayer, meditation, self-giving, inti-

[14] Ibid.

macy with God, fidelity to the Holy Spirit, and the conviction that Christ, and not we ourselves, is the architect and builder of the kingdom.[15]

This is an intriguing thought, for as the agenda belongs to God, the task itself belongs to God, for it is by the guidance of the Spirit of God. Consider Acts 13.1–3 for a moment. In that passage Luke described the worship and fasting of many within the church at Antioch. During their assembly, the Holy Spirit instructed, "Set apart for me Barnabas and Saul for the work which I have called them" (2). Following the Spirit's instruction they laid their hands on these two men and sent them to begin their work.

A couple significant things emerge from the passage. First, Barnabas and Saul were separated from the rest for the purpose of the Holy Spirit: "Set apart for me…" Second, these men were about to do a work they had been called by the Spirit to do. The Spirit made it very clear that the choice of and the task set before these two men were not of human orientation, but were entirely divine: they had been called to do what the Spirit of God called his own.

Paul reminded the elders of the church in Ephesus that they had been made[16] overseers[17] by the Holy Spirit. Recognizing the gravity of this event—a task that belonged to God and a calling or making that belonged to the Spirit of God—Paul's reminder is significant. Their calling and making as elders were not the result of anything human oriented, but divine in every way. Their task, to care for the flock, was founded upon the fact that the flock belonged to God and so therefore their responsibility was to God first, and then to those that God claimed as his own.

---

[15] Shawchuck and Heuser, *Leading the Congregation*, 123.

[16] From *etheto*, a form of *tithemi*, "to set in an arrangement or position."

[17] The Greek, *presbuterous*, "elder, senior, someone older."

Third: Care for the Church. A third element of Paul's challenge to the elders in Ephesus is that their task was to "care for the church of God," being aware of the threat of the "fierce wolves" that come soon after Paul's departure, "not sparing the flock." The first part, caring for the church, is rather obvious and straightforward; servant leaders must care for the congregation as a whole through nurture, guidance, and motivation. In his characteristics/qualifications of elders Paul indicated that part of their task was to care for their congregation (1 Tim. 3.5). As Paul listed his experiences and sufferings in his ministry, he concluded the list with his anxiety ("deep concern," NKJV; "concern," NIV; "anxiety," RSV) over the churches (2 Cor. 11.28).

I want to address, however, the second part, the threat of "fierce" (as rendered in the ESV and RSV) or "savage"(NIV and NKJV) wolves. It has been assumed perhaps that these wolves only included the false teachers and trouble-makers from among the Jews and within the churches, such as Diotrophes (3 John 9–10), those who had bewitched the Galatian churches (Gal. 1.6–9; 3.1), those with "itching ears" who did not accept sound doctrine (2 Tim. 4.3–4), and perhaps Demas (2 Tim. 4.10). There is no doubt that such people were in Paul's mind as he lodged this warning to the elders of the church in Ephesus. At the same time, however, concern must be for those who might be led astray by these wolves. Picture in your mind the sentries in the watchtowers diligently searching the landscape for the approach of danger. They watch intently for any movement, any threat that may emerge from the shadows or come rushing in from hidden places. Yet, while they so diligently scan the landscape, those that they are seeking to protect leave the safety of the fortress to wander about within the grasp of those who would harm them. It is one thing to watch for danger as it approaches, but it is also another thing to make sure those within the walls remain there and safe.

Fourth: Passionately Admonish. A fourth and final element that I notice in Paul's challenge to the elders in Ephesus was that they were to "be alert" and, as Paul did, admonish the congregation passionately ("with tears"). Dedication to the task and to the organization as a whole must be paramount to all leaders. If a sense of passion for what they must accomplish does not dominate their thinking, leaders can become distracted from their greater task, acting as the stewards and servants of what belongs to God. That may be behind Paul's association of "tears" with the urgency and passion of being alert caretakers of God's people.

An understanding of servant leadership is important because there are fundamental misunderstandings of what leaders/elders are to do; what their function and place truly are. That misunderstanding manifests itself perhaps in the assumption that being a leader assumes being in control and that being in control means to be dominating and overbearing. These assumptions perhaps convey images of the military officer dominating and manipulating new recruits. It is assumed that congregational health and betterment demand a clearly defined hierarchy: i.e., the elders are in charge and everyone else is subordinate. While a sense of being in control is both biblical and necessary for effective leadership, there is a misunderstanding of how that control is both defined and implemented. The misunderstanding is due in part to a misapplication of the biblical idea of terms such as "rule" (cf. 1 Tim. 3.4–5). It is assumed by some that being in charge, being in control, means to be dominant and intimidating.

Many years ago, an elder of a congregation described an incident that had occurred a few years earlier. The preacher of the congregation had information regarding some of the congregation's evangelistic efforts and informed two of the elders he would like to meet with them on a given day to share and discuss it. The elder relating this incident to me took great pride in informing the preacher that he, the preacher, did not decide when meetings would be called and he, the preacher, did not decide what information should be presented. That was the duty of the elders and only the elders, he proclaimed. That elder, I feel, failed to see the bigger picture of leadership. It is granted that leaders must decide, leaders must orchestrate, and leaders must manage—they must do so or else they will lose control and authority—but I feel he failed to understand the nature of informed leadership and the ability to be in control through the input of others.

It is forgotten, far too often perhaps, that leaders in the church are servants—both to the Lord and to others—as are any of the other members of the Lord's church. If in no other way, this is borne out through the statement of "qualifications" for elders and deacons in 1 Tim. 3 and Titus 1. They must observe their task as obedient servants of the Lord. Consider Paul's statement that elders are to care for the church of God (1 Tim. 3.5). Consider also that the word rendered "rule" in the KJV, NKJV, and perhaps other translations is from the original, *proistemi*, meaning "to be a leader, to have authority over, to manage," or "to care for," as in Titus 3.8. While there is certainly the place for authority and the need to lead and manage, the sentiment is one of service, not domination. J.W. McGarvey emphasized that elders are leaders, in part, by the example that they set.[18] Citing John 10.4, which speaks of the shepherd going before his sheep so that they may follow him, McGarvey commented, "There is no driving, but constant leading. A Judean shepherd going before his flock and calling them with a voice which they know and always follow,

---

[18] J.W. McGarvey, *A Treatise on the Eldership* (Chillocothe, OH: Deward Publishing Company, 2010), 31.

is an inimitably beautiful picture of the chief Shepherd himself, and of all the under shepherds, leading their flocks toward the gates of heaven."[19] The ideas of being "alert" and "tears" go well with the task of leaders who are servants to the Lord and to the congregation they lead. Consider the implications of Paul's encouragement in 1 Timothy 5.17, "Let the elders who rule well be considered worthy of double honor…" I am intrigued by the term "rule well" (ESV, NKJV, RSV; the NIV renders it, "direct the affairs of the church well").

If the leaders of the church are going to rule well so as to receive double honor, they must be on guard, and so then alert. As stewards of what belongs to God, they must keep the church as the Lord intended it. McGarvey considered the task of being alert to the wolves that prey against the church a part of shepherding.[20] He alludes to Jesus' parable of the lost sheep (John 15.3–7) as an example of such care and alertness. Admittedly, McGarvey's allusion to the parable primarily addresses those times when "a disciple strays away from the path of duty" and the elders must "go and hunt up, and try to win back, the wanderer."[21] At the same time, however, this is a part of the larger task of such alertness to the approach of the wolves: not only keeping them at bay, but keeping the vulnerable sheep safe and secure.

Jesus: The Best Example

Greenleaf would probably agree that he was by no means the originator of the concept of servant leadership. I have already mentioned that his inspiration for the servant as leader arose from the role of Leo in Hesses' *Journey to the East*:

---

[19] Ibid., 30.
[20] Ibid., 33.
[21] Ibid., 34.

In this story we see a band of men on a mythical journey...The central figure of the story is Leo, who accompanies the party as the servant who does their menial chores, but also sustains them with his spirit and his song. He is a person of extraordinary presence. All goes well until Leo disappears. Then the group falls into disarray and the journey is abandoned. They cannot make it without the servant Leo. The narrator, one of the party, after some years of wandering, finds Leo and is taken into the Order that had sponsored the journey. There he discovers that Leo, whom he had known first as a servant, was in fact the titular head of the Order, its guiding spirit, a great and noble leader.[22]

Greenleaf found inspiration in the character of Leo who became a voice of prophecy; that the "theory of prophecy...that the voices of great clarity," wrote Greenleaf, "are speaking cogently all of the time."[23] For Greenleaf, the example of Leo became one of those prophetic voices.

As with all things essential to the human experience, it is the Bible that launched this foundational and fundamental methodology, and it is the Bible that reveals Jesus Christ as the greatest example of servant leadership ever to be found. In His practice of ministry, He epitomized the very essence of humility and a positive example of a servant. Paul offered that Jesus, even though in the form of God, humbled himself in the form of a servant through obedience (Phil. 2.5–8).

When the disciples argued over who would be regarded as the greatest, Jesus responded by reminding them of many things they had obviously forgotten or failed to hear:

> A dispute also arose among them, as to which of them was to be regarded as the greatest. And he said to them, "The kings of the Gentiles exercise lordship over them, and those in authority over

---

[22] Greenleaf, *Servant Leadership*, 21.
[23] Ibid., 22.

them are called benefactors. But not so with you. Rather, let the greatest among you become as the youngest, and the leader as one who serves. For who is the greater, one who reclines at table or one who serves? Is it not the one who reclines at table? But I am among you as the one who serves. You are those who have stayed with me in my trials, [29] and I assign to you, as my Father assigned to me, a kingdom, [30] that you may eat and drink at my table in my kingdom and sit on thrones judging the twelve tribes of Israel" (Lk. 22.24–30).

Jesus reminded His disciples that their concerns were of the world—lordship and authority. He had something better in mind for them, however, that was founded service and humility. He asked them who is greater: the one who reclines at the table or the one who serves. Of course, common sense would indicate the one who reclines at the table; the one being served is the greater. His answer dropped a bombshell on their perceptions when he responded that it is the one who serves that is the greater with His statement, "But I am among you as the one who serves" (27).

Jesus became the greatest example of the servant, and so the servant leader and His message reversed what was common knowledge. Strauch wrote, "The servant leadership that Jesus taught and modeled stood in opposition to that of the religious leaders who were obsessed with special privileges, status, and honorific titles."[24] Jesus' message was one of humility and service to others rather than the obtaining of power, position, and titles.

Jesus spoke of leadership, as well as the servant who is a leader, throughout his ministry. In the Old Testament the Hebrew *'eved* was associated with being a slave but could also be an identification of a trusted servant, someone who did work for a ruler or king.[25] Isaiah wrote of those who acted as servants of God as well

---

[24] Strauch, *Meetings That Work*, 22–23.

[25] Howard Young, "Rediscovering Servant Leadership" (2002), *Enrichment*

as servants of others (42.1–4; 49.1–6; 50.4–9; 52.13–53.12). Jesus alluded to the Hebrew Scriptures throughout his ministry in regard to servants and servant leaders. In Luke 4, Jesus entered the synagogue at Nazareth and was asked to read. The text reveals that he unrolled the scroll, found a certain place and began to read, "The Spirit of the Lord is upon me, because he has anointed me to proclaim good news to the poor. He has sent me to proclaim liberty to the captives and recovering of sight to the blind, to set at liberty those who are oppressed, to proclaim the year of the Lord's favor" (Luke 4.18–19; cf. Is. 61.1,2). To be sure, the word "servant" is not used in this passage, but the implications are clear. Jesus, as the Christ, Messiah and Lord, was to be sent out, according to prophecy, as the servant who would announce good things (news) to the poor, the captive, the blind, and the oppressed. Such a scene is reminiscent of the servant in the marriage feast parables to announce the commencement of the celebration and to invite the guest to who agree to come (cf. Matt.22.3, 8–10; Luke 14.17).

While on their way to Capernaum, the disciples of Jesus argued who would be the greatest among them (Mark 9.33–34). He said to them, "If anyone would be first, he must be last of all and servant of all" (35). For Jesus, to be a servant was to be humble with no concern for greatness, esteem, and social place. Recall that in this setting, he was speaking to those who would be leaders in the growth of the church that the Lord would establish upon his divine foundation (cf. Matt. 16.13–18). If they were to be those leaders, they had to become servants in heart and practice. This intentional example of and teaching about service saturated the ministry of Jesus and formed a framework of humility, sacrifice, and suffering that would be revealed over and over in the unfolding history of the church within the New Testament.

Journal: Enriching and Equipping Spirit-Filled Ministers, page 2 .http://enrichmentjournal.ag.org/200202/200202_ 032_serv_leader.cfm.

Effective and biblical leadership is found in the servant-leader model exemplified by Jesus and the practice of servant leadership is displayed best, in my opinion, in an incredible story within the ministry of Jesus in John 13. In this passage is the wonderful story of Jesus washing the disciples' feet. The story is simple. Jesus and his disciples reclined together in the upper room on Thursday evening to begin the Passover meal, what Jesus referred to "as a harbinger of the messianic feast he would enjoy with them in the consummated kingdom."[26] This event became the conclusion to three years of Jesus' empowerment and equipping of his disciples in preparation for the conclusion of his own ministry and the beginning of their own. Instigating this modified Passover meal, "Jesus bequeathed to his disciples one final visual lesson."[27]

After they had eaten the Passover meal, Jesus removed His outer clothing and began to wash the feet of each of the disciples assembled with Him. Peter, at first, refused to allow the Lord to do this but, upon Jesus' insistence, requested Jesus wash his head, hands, and feet. When the task was finished, Jesus asked them if they understood what He had just done. Ever the Teacher, Jesus said that if He, Lord and Savior, would wash their feet, then they should wash one another's feet. Howell summarized the point: "[Jesus] made the application clear through a greater to lesser argument: If I have done this for you, how much more should you do this for one another (13.12–14). Jesus, rightly elevated as Teacher and Lord and Sender, set his disciples an example (13.15) by serving them so they, mere students and servants and messengers, might prove their identification with him by serving one another."[28] As Drury wrote, "The Church of the man who wrapped a towel about Himself to wash His own disciples' feet

---

[26] Howell, *Servant of the Servant*, 201.

[27] Ibid.

[28] Ibid.

as His final lesson to them certainly cannot reject servant leadership as a proper approach to leading others."[29]

It is upon that foundation that servant-leadership is based: the desire to lead through service to others and not through domination and intimidation. Too often this is not the case, for some congregational leaders see themselves as the ultimate authority of the congregation, when they are actually servants of He who has all authority in heaven and earth (cf. Mt. 28.18). So, they feel themselves to be the primary force within the congregation: their authority; their congregation; their plan; their programs. They are not to be questioned and what they decide must be done. This occurs, I believe, due to a misunderstanding of their role as leaders, managers, and shepherds. An analogy I offer is of a single man who is suddenly given the care and safety of fifteen four-year-old children. Faced with the task, what will he want to do first? Usually, take control; let them know the rules; let them know who is in charge, when, instead, he should make sure the children are safe and cared for.

Do not misunderstand; I am not insisting leaders are not to be in charge, even dominating when circumstances dictate. To be sure, they are the shepherds, so they must shepherd. As Psalm 23 implies, that stresses leading, deciding, directing, protecting, as well as caring and nurturing. They are also to be dominant, but not dominating; they are to dictate, but not be dictators. Paul told the elders at Ephesus they were "overseers, to shepherd the church of God" (Acts 20.28). They had the responsibility to watch for "savage wolves" who would not "spare the flock." That is an awesome responsibility and a daunting task, one that takes servants and not controllers. They must be servants of the Lord and of the people, not manipulators.

Paul also instructed the elders on Crete (through Titus) toward their task (Titus 1.10–16). They were to stop the mouths

---

[29] Drury, *Handbook*, 22.

of the insubordinate, idle talkers, and deceivers. He instructed, "Therefore, rebuke them sharply, that they may be sound in the faith" (13). They had the responsibility of keeping deceit and trouble out. That is difficult and takes courage. It means they must take control, but not be controlling; be leaders, but leaders who serve. Without the hearts of able servants, they cannot do this. There is a difference between being in charge and being overbearing; there is a difference between being dominating and being dictatorial.

A key element of leadership in the church is servanthood[30]—the desire to be a servant of the Lord and of the people. Consider a passage not usually associated with this. In Gal. 5.13, Paul wrote, "For you brethren have been called to liberty; only do not use liberty as an opportunity for the flesh, but through love serve one another." The context of the passage is love and not opposition. I find v. 13 very significant, for it reminds us of two important things. First, there is the function of liberty—freedom, the misuse of it and its proper place and use. Diotrophes is an example, for he loved to have the preeminence, used malicious words, and was guilty of manipulation and control (3 Jn. 9–10). A key misuse of liberty is to believe it allows what it does not. Second, there is the connection of love and being a servant to others. If we are to love the Lord and His church, we will then serve Him and His church. If we are to love our brothers and sisters, we will therefore serve them.

At first blush, at the very beginning, in the first light of understanding congregational leadership, it must be understood that it begins with the heart of the servant! So much is still to be determined. For example, more research is demanded to determine its spiritual and moral-ethical emphases. Some have done much to

---

[30] When I was writing this my computer's spell check function did not like the word "servanthood," yet the word will stand as written.

contribute to the study (Barbuto & Wheeler, 2006; Senjaya, Sarros, & Santora, 2008), and a few (e.g. Laub, 2004) have sought to bridge the gap and determine the validity, or lack thereof, of servant leadership. More, however, much more, needs to be done.

I believe servant leadership as a biblical concept is so much better articulated and discernable than its secular cousin. Its place and function in spiritual leadership is found in the ministry of Jesus and in the lives of the characters in both the Old and New Testament, and is voiced in the development and work of the church of the New Testament through servants such as the apostle Paul and so many others.

THREE | *Followership*

As children, we played a game called "follow the leader." Basically, it was a game of challenges where the participants were expected to follow another player, the leader, doing what he or she did and going where he or she went. That very simple childhood game carried with it a very simple but significant point: someone must lead and others must follow.

In scholarly leadership research, the subject of followership has not always been a target study, for it is "an understudied discipline."[1] This gap is surprising, for in the business and military world it would appear to be an obvious concern. I would also think the educational world would be more accepting of followership as a serious topic of research due to the teacher-student dynamic.[2] In regard to the subject of congregational and spiritual leadership, the study of followership would seem more appealing perhaps if understood for what it is: a study of connections, associations, and relationships in the larger dynamic

---

[1] Kent Bjugstad, Elizabeth C. Thach, Karen Thompson, and Alan Morris. "A Fresh Look at Followership: A Model for Matching Followership and Leadership Styles. *Institute of Behavioral and Applied Management* (2006): 304.

[2] I am not a student of business, military or education leadership except through some encounters in my studies of organizational leadership. This statement is, therefore, an assumption.

of leadership and how the leader-follower relationship works in a congregation.

Why is followership so understudied? The answer may be relevant to a major problem in organizational concerns; that leaders, not followers, are of central focus. Don Grayson and Ryan Speckhart wrote, "Today's society is inclined to place leadership on a pedestal."[3] In 1990, Lundin and Lancaster added, "America's passionate and unremitting love affair with leadership shows little sign of waning."[4] Indeed, evidence of this abounds. We praise the corporate leader who takes the fledging and/or struggling company and builds it into a global power, even though he or she could not possibly do so alone. It is Patton and the Battle of the Bulge, the MVP of the Super Bowl, the coach of the year, and other distinguished leaders who could not have accomplished what they did without their staff, employees, associates, and teammates.

Don Mercer commented, "There is a built in assumption in our society that everybody should strive to be a leader."[5] This assumption, in part, acknowledges why followership takes a back seat to leadership. To achieve something worthwhile is to become a leader; to be a follower is to underachieve. Ira Chaleff put it rather succinctly when he wrote, "We are a society in love with leadership and uncomfortable with followership, though the subjects are inseparable. We don't honor followership. We talk pejoratively of followers being weak individuals. And we certainly don't train staff how to be strong followers who are not only capa-

---

[3] Don Grayson and Ryan Speckhart, (2006). "The leader-follower relationship: Practitioner Observations." *Leadership Advance Online* VI (Winter): 1.

[4] Stephen C. Lundin, and Lynne C. Lancaster (1990) "Beyond Leadership...The Importance of Followership" in *Futurist* 24.3 (May/June 1990): 18.

[5] Don Mercer, "Followership: the Corollary to Leadership," *Todd Nielson* (March 20, 2012): 1. http://www. Toddnielson.com/followership-the-corollary-to-leadership.

ble of brilliantly supporting their leaders, but can also effectively stand up to them when their actions or policies are detrimental and need rethinking."[6] Chaleff rightly pointed out the mistake of ignoring the significance and importance of the leader-follower relationship.

In the movie, *Reign of Fire*, the character Denton Van Zan at first exhibits a very arrogant attitude toward Quinn Abercromby: "I lead, you follow," he commands. As Van Zan learns from his mistakes through the loss of his friend, Creedy, due to his arrogance, his attitude changes to the point where he informs Abercromby, "You lead, I follow." Van Zan learned that the leader and the follower often share responsibility and that both are key to success.

The emergence of the field of followership as a topic of research and praxis has been attributed to Robert Kelley, but followership research was most likely introduced by Mary Parker Follett (Sept. 3, 1868–Dec. 18, 1933), an incredible individual who "paved the way for the contemporary study of power authority, and influence in business, in the private sector. To her it was a study "of the utmost importance, but which has been far too little considered."[7] Follett challenged her readers to focus on the meaning of leadership instead of the actual leader. Unfortunately, Follett had to wait half a century to receive the full credit and recognition she deserved.[8] Other research has followed more recently, such as in the work of Bain and Strebel on follower motivations;[9] Hanges,

---

[6] Ira Chaleff. (2001). "Courageous Followers, Courageous Leaders," *Ideas for Leaders* (December): 1.

[7] Bjugstad, et al., "A Fresh Look at Followership," 304.

[8] Leadership Readings Responses (September 22, 2012). http://leadforsocialchange. wordpress.com/2012/09/22/mary-parker-follett-the-essentials-of-leadership.

[9] D. Bain. (1982). *The productivity prescription* New York: McGraw-Hill. P. Strebel. (1996). "Why do employees resist change?" *Harvard Business Review*

Offerman, and Day, and Ehrhart and Klein on follower values and trust,[10] and Bennis, and Gilbert and Hyde regarding effective and ineffective followers.[11] [12]

Servant leadership is a model focused on the relationship of two or more individuals with one functioning as the leader and others functioning as followers. Greenleaf observed effectively the relationship:

> Leadership means that one individual has a better than average sense of what should be done now and is willing to take the risk to say, 'Let us do this now.' The process of consensus is followed up to the point where some individual must take this risk—this leap of faith. Spontaneous consensus rarely goes to the point of clearly indicating action. Inspiration is usually received by the best prepared individual who, for this immediate act, is the leader....Followership is an equally responsible role because it means that the individual must take the risk to empower the leader and to say, in the matter at hand, 'I will trust your insight.' Followership implies another preparation in order that trusting,

---

74, 86–92.

[10] P. Hanges, L. Offerman, and D. Day. (2001). "Leaders, followers and values: Progress and prospects for theory and research. *Leadership Quarterly* 12, 129–131. M.G. Ehrhart and K.J. Klein. (2001). "Predicting follower's preferences for charismatic leadership: The influence of follower values and personality. *Leadership Quarterly* 45, 5.

[11] W. Bennis. (2000). *Managing the Dream: Reflections on Leadership and Change.* Cambridge, MA: Perseus Books. R.G. Gilbert and A.C. Hyde. (1998). "Followership and the federal worker." *Public Administration Review* 48, 962–968.

[12] It is not the thesis of this book to examine the minutiae of Kelley's breakdown of followership, or any of the deeper research within the scholarship of the study. This book is intended to be a popular examination of leadership studies and the value of the servant-leader model in congregational leadership. I will, however, offer a brief look from time to time of where the deeper research is going. Kelley's study distinguished two different styles of followers: independent, critical thinking which is seen as either alienated or effective followership, and dependent, uncritical thinking which is seen as either passive or conformist followership.

empowering the leader, will be a strength-giving element in the institution....Both leading and following, in an institution that becomes a thing of beauty because of the serving power that is generated, require of all a common purpose and a clear definition of obligations. Where the obligations are not precisely defined and willingly accepted, the basis of trust cannot exist.[13]

Greenleaf addressed the basis of the leader-follower relationship, one of trust and obligation. The leader's responsibility is to lead and the follower's responsibility is to follow. That simple fact must be understood and embraced.

It is therefore essential to realize the value and function of both the leader and the follower(s), for without the one, the other cannot exist. In other words, one cannot lead unless one or more will follow, and one cannot follow unless there is a leader. This very simple but true dynamic, the reciprocal nature of leader-follower, is a basis of the leader-follower relationship. Trudy Heller and Jon Van Til wrote in their propositional article, "Leadership and Followership," of the connection of the leader-follower relationship: "Leadership and followership are linked concepts, neither of which can be comprehended without understanding the other."[14]

So then, it is a mistake to view leadership as superior in place or function over followership, and this is especially true within the congregation. Drury wrote, "Church leaders must be people-developers more than program pushers. The church-based servant leader starts with the people, not the program. People development is the church's product."[15] In other words, what true servant leaders—indeed, true leaders in general—do is not about them or their position, but about their place and function within the

---

[13] Greenleaf, *Servant Leadership*, 256.

[14] Trudy Heller and Jon Van Til (1982). "Leadership and Followership: Some Summary Propositions," *Journal of Applied Behavioral Science* 18, 405.

[15] Drury, *Handbook*, 22.

leader-follower relationship. In this way, leadership is not a position to attain, nor an accolade to receive, but a responsibility as a leader who seeks the development of the whole: elders who seek to develop the congregation.

The idea of the leader-follower relationship is seen well in the biblical imagery of the shepherd and the sheep where the "linked concepts" Heller and Van Til described are seen wonderfully in the shepherd-sheep relationship (cf. John 10). Just as reciprocity is necessary within the secular view of leader-follower, so it is found within the model of shepherd-sheep: one cannot exist without the other, for a shepherd cannot function without his flock, and the flock cannot function without the shepherd.

Consider the shepherd-sheep model in light of Psalm 23. While the psalm is very familiar to those inside and outside of biblical studies, it is often under-estimated and under-appreciated for its depth and power. Often assigned to sermon illustrations and appreciated as little more than a comfort text by funeral homes, the psalm is a clear and significant theological statement of the Christ as divine Lord and spiritual Shepherd.

> The LORD is my shepherd; I shall not want.
>   He makes me lie down in green pastures.
> He leads me beside still waters.
>   He restores my soul.
> He leads me in paths of righteousness
>   for his name's sake.
>
> Even though I walk through the valley of the shadow of death,
>   I will fear no evil,
> for you are with me;
>   your rod and your staff,
>   they comfort me.
>
> You prepare a table before m
>   in the presence of my enemies;

> you anoint my head with oil;
>> my cup overflows.
> Surely goodness and mercy shall follow me
>> all the days of my life,
> and I shall dwell in the house of the LORD
>> forever.

The psalm is, of course, a Christological treatise of the divine Shepherd, manifested through the incarnation, ministry, and mission of Jesus Christ. As the divine Shepherd, Christ is our spiritual sustainer ("green pastures;" "still waters;" "my cup overflows;"), our spiritual guide ("paths of righteousness;" "valley of the shadow of death....you are with me;"), our spiritual comforter ("rod and staff...a table...in the presence of my enemies;" "anoint my head with oil;", and our spiritual assurance ("surely goodness and mercy...house of the Lord forever").

The psalm is also a proclamation of the leader-follower, shepherd-sheep relationship. As the shepherd/leader, his role does not exist without the sheep/followers. In other words, he cannot shepherd or lead without sheep/followers to benefit from it; he cannot provide without sheep/followers to receive. At the same time, the sheep/followers have no direction or sustaining without their shepherd/leader. John 10.4 once again helps us with this: "When he has brought out all his own, he goes before them, and the sheep follow him, for they know his voice." Such is the shepherd-sheep, leader-follower relationship. The shepherd leads and the sheep follow; the sheep has needs to be met and the shepherd provides for those needs.

I will add a point to this brief consideration of the twenty-third psalm. In a study of congregational eldership, Psalm 23 must be a central, focal point of concern. Most studies focus on 1 Timothy 3 and Titus 1, and I have already mentioned the need to include Acts

20 in the study, as well. Psalm 23, however, must have a strong voice in understanding the biblical model of effective, efficient leadership. Within the psalm are the characteristics of a shepherd/leader:

- Responsibility—leading to green pastures and still waters; guidance and security in the valley of the shadow of death; a table in presence of enemies
- Compassion—rod and staff
- Support and recognition—anoint head with oil; cup runs over
- Hope for future—dwell in house of the Lord forever

Key to understanding and embracing the shepherd-sheep/leader-follower relationship is the ability and desire for the shepherd/leader to provide for the sheep/followers. As Jones wrote, "Leadership is always about serving the highest priority needs of those who are being led."[16]

Follow the Leader and Reciprocity

The leader-follower relationship is, among other things, about reciprocity, and every leader and follower must understand and embrace this reciprocal element. *Webster's New Collegiate Dictionary* defines "followership" very simply but concisely as "the capacity or willingness to follow a leader."[17] At first glance, this definition might appear to be too simple in its scope, but a closer examination reveals two significant points. First, followership involves and even demands a willingness to follow. Heller and Van Til proposed, "The leader must lead, and do it well to retain leadership; the follower must follow, and do it well to retain followership."[18] Why is this important? To merely follow someone is not the same as being willing to do so. For example, one might

---

[16] Jones, *Heart, Mind, and Strength*, 13.

[17] *Webster's New Collegiate Dictionary*, 1973, p. 446 .

[18] Heller and Van Til, "Leadership and Followership," 407.

follow another only because he or she must do so. The pecking order found within the military or within the business world are two examples. In those settings, the expectation and even the demand to follow might not elicit a willingness to do so. Followership would then be the result of subordinate expectations, even coercion from those of a superior level of authority. One follows only because he or she has no other choice; his or her function within that dynamic is to do what he or she is told according to the expectations of those in authority over him or her.

That point leads to the second reason *Webster's* definition of followership is significant. Followership involves the recognition of others who possess greater authority. As stated earlier, someone must lead and someone must follow, and both must understand their function within that relational dynamic. Organizations, congregations included, fail to function properly and effectively when this dynamic is not recognized, embraced, and utilized.

What does this look like? Put simply, leaders, by the definition of their function within the organization, demand that followers follow. On the other hand, followers must know that their leader(s) will lead. In the movie *Master and Commander: The Far Side of the World*[19] with Russell Crowe, the captain of an English warship during the Napoleonic Wars strives to not only defeat the French navy, but also equip and empower his young and maturing officers, as well the crew. One of the officers, a young lord who is small and had lost an arm in battle, rises superbly to lead others, even those who are much older and more seasoned. Another young lord cannot seem to lead as his captain expects, but remains indecisive and weak. At the end of the day, he acts only when someone else of greater decisiveness suggests a plan of action. The former young lord was a leader who expected those he must lead

---

[19] Peter Weir, director. November 14, 2003. http://www.imdb.com/title/tt0311113/combined.

to follow, which they do upon his command. The latter young lord was not a leader because he would not lead.

The need to understand the functional aspect of the leader-follower dynamic—that the leader must lead and the follower must follow—is seen, again, in the biblical model of the shepherd and his sheep. Jesus said:

> Truly, truly, I say to you, he who does not enter the sheepfold by the door but climbs in by another way, that man is a thief and a robber. But he who enters by the door is the shepherd of the sheep. To him the gatekeeper opens. The sheep hear his voice, and he calls his own sheep by name and leads them out. When he has brought out all his own, he goes before them, and the sheep follow him, for they know his voice. A stranger they will not follow, but they will flee from him, for they do not know the voice of strangers (John 10.1–5).

In this passage, Jesus describes the "voice" of the shepherd as the voice of command and direction which guides and comforts the sheep: "The sheep hear his voice, and he calls his own sheep by name and leads them out." Reciprocity is demonstrated in this passage through a simple dynamic seen most frequently in the business world: supply and demand. The sheep have various demands (hearing the shepherd's voice; he calls them by name; a shepherd to follow) and the shepherd supplies their needs (he is the true shepherd, for he enters by the door; he calls out with his voice; he leads the sheep). Leaders and followers must understand and embrace that they work as a part of a larger team, an organization with a specific set of goals and agendas. As parts of the larger team or organization, the leader-follower relationship is one of reciprocity[20] where each gives back and enhances the other.

---

[20] Reciprocity is defined as "the condition of being reciprocal" and reciprocal is defined as "in return; mutual; expressing mutual action or relation;" *Oxford Illustrated American Dictionary* (London, New York, Sydney, Moscow: DK Publishing, Inc., 1998), 683.

Examples of such reciprocity and team-oriented thinking abound. I am a sports enthusiast, so I will use a sports-related illustration. In the world of professional basketball, emphasis is placed more often than not on the individual players—Wilt Chamberlain, "Magic" Johnson, Kareem Abdul-Jabbar, Michael Jordan, LeBron James, and so on. The same might be said of a professional baseball team—Mickey Mantle, Babe Ruth, Reggie Jackson, Hank Aaron, and Johnny Bench, for example. In reality, a basketball and baseball team must function as a multi-member collective, working together for the same purpose. Those teams, however, must function with a sense of reciprocity, as well. As they move the ball up the court or take the field, each player must assume his or her respective role in the game plan, working in synchronization, and focusing on the same goal. Such teamwork and reciprocity leads to success. It is teamwork because they function as a unit, as a whole; it is reciprocal because what each individual does benefits, enhances and assists the efforts of the others.

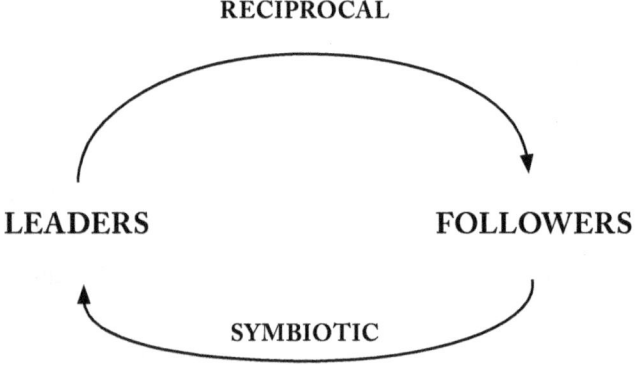

Fig. 1- Leader-Follower Reciprocity/Symbiosis

Within the sphere of reciprocity it must be understood that leadership and followership inform one another. In their functioning as a team the leader-follower relationship functions in part through feeding off of one another. As I will explain a bit later, this feeding relationship becomes a cyclical thing: each side moving and working from the input and function of the other.

An effective leader-follower dynamic is also symbiotic, which is defined as, "living together in more or less intimate association or close union of two dissimilar organisms; the intimate living together of two dissimilar organisms in a mutually beneficial relationship."[21] In nature, symbiosis is seen in relationships such as that of the tick birds that sit on the back of a rhinoceros or the remora that swim with sharks. The birds clean the rhino's hide of ticks, the remora clean the shark of parasites, and the hide of the hippo and the skin of the shark provides a source of food. Other examples abound, including the clown fish that lives within the poisonous barbs of the sea anemone, monkeys as they groom one another, and the bumble bee pollinating a flowering plant. Nature provides a wonderful example of the beneficial element of a symbiotic relationship.

I associate the element of symbiosis with the leader-follower dynamic because not only is the relationship to be reciprocal, it can also be symbiotic, for the leader is beneficial to the follower and the follower is beneficial to the leader. For example, the leader might provide guidance and a clear vision for the follower(s) to implement, while the followers provide the essential work and implementation the leader requires for the task to be completed. In congregational leadership, such reciprocity and symbiosis are significant in the leader-follower, shepherd-member/worker relationship.

A significant part of reciprocal and symbiotic relationships is a co-existence of trust and reliability. This is a biblical concept, to be sure. In 1 Timothy 3.4 Paul emphasized the responsibility of shepherds to "manage" (ESV, NASV, RSV, NIV) or "care" (KJV, NKJV), rendered from the original *prostenai*, a form of *proistemi*

---

[21] Webster's New Collegiate Dictionary, 1973, p. 1180.

meaning to have authority over, manage, or care for something. To the elders of the Ephesian church, Paul instructed them to pay attention ("take heed," KJV, RSV, NKJV; "keep watch," NIV) to themselves and the flock, "to care for the church of God" (ESV), derived from *"prosechete,"* meaning to pay attention to something, to be watchful and on guard. It is clear from these passages that Paul intended the shepherds to be reliable and trustworthy as caretakers of the congregation; that the congregation could depend upon them for such care.

The congregational part in this reciprocal/symbiotic relationship is somewhat less evident in Scripture, but significant points are found here and there. For example, in 1 Timothy 5.19 Paul instructs Timothy and the Ephesian church not to bring a charge or accusation against an elder unless it is through two or three witnesses. Peter instructed the younger within the scattered churches to "be subject to the elders" (1 Pet. 5.5). Trustworthiness, dependability, and reliability are also expected from the congregation, the followers of the leaders.

In such a relationship, the elders/shepherds and the members/workers are able to do what they are expected to do. In other words, it allows the supervisors to supervise and the workers to work. This is difficult when the leaders are unhappy trusting others to carry out what has been planned, or when the followers/workers are unhappy only doing the work. We see this type of problem arise when one or more of the elders feel he/they must micromanage every step of anything that is planned, or when the members of the congregation become disgruntled because they can only do the work necessary to carry out a given plan. This type of logjam to effective work is crippling to any organization's future success, including a congregation.[22] Nothing really ever gets done effectively and efficiently because, as the saying goes, there are too many

---

[22] I will address issues such as implementation, trust, and delegation later.

cooks in the kitchen. The leader-follower relationship understands who will lead/supervise/guide and who will follow/work.

A model that I use to illustrate this essential element of this relationship is what I call the Feeding/Providing Model (Fig. 2). The feeding/providing model is concerned with trust and results, primarily. In other words, the leader trusts his or her followers/workers to properly implement the task he or she has designed, and the followers/workers trust the leader to provide them with what they need to accomplish their assigned task. So then, the leader(s) will feed the followers/workers with supplies, proper instruction, and guidance, and the followers/workers would provide the leader(s) with proper results, as well as expertise and experience in doing the task. So, reciprocally and symbiotically, each side of the task provides and feeds the other.

THE FEEDING/PROVIDING MODEL

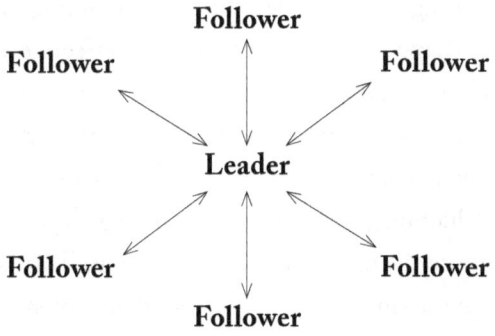

Fig. 2- The Feeding/Providing Model

One way the feeding/providing model is seen at work is in a production factory. From the CEO/president to the vice-presidents to the engineers/designers/draftsmen to the supervisors to the foremen to the line workers to the lowest-level laborers, work is accomplished through the combined efforts of leadership and followership at various levels. The CEO/president, vice-presidents, supervisors, foremen, and even the workers/laborers provide a form of leadership, each doing what they are trained and designated to do, while each level also provides what is needed for the others to accomplish their tasks.

In the study of leadership, the feeding/providing model reveals the productive connection between the leaders and followers, and so the elders and the congregation within a congregation. In this way, the elders establish what is to be done and then provide the congregation the means by which it can be accomplished. In return, the congregation implements and develops the elders' plan. Each side provides both leadership and implementation, feeding and providing for each other.

Why is feeding and providing so important? Consider the example of a company that designs and builds tubular-steel frames. The company was the brain-child of the president of the company, who started the business in his garage. He was the only employee at first, developing an effective method of bending tubular steel, designing the shape of the frame, the most effective way to weld the joints and connections, and the best way to powder-coat the finished product. As the company grows, the originator and owner of the company becomes its president, but he cannot let go of the hands-on production of the frames, insisting on overseeing and even participating in each stage of production. This is done even though the president/owner has hired department supervisors, production foremen, laborers, and salesmen. The result is a company with employees with expertise and experience who cannot contribute to the development of its product and cannot take any sort of lead, at any level, in the company's future itself. There is no feeding and providing between the leader and the employees, so no sense of ownership or accomplishment is felt. Feeding and providing allows both leadership and followership to contribute to the purpose and function of the organization.

What does this look like within a congregation? I recently read a vision statement of an eldership as they presented it to the congregation they serve. In that statement, they provided a view of the future which included spiritual and numerical growth, ministry, evangelism, education, and missions. It also included their acceptance of their role as the shepherds of the congregation as visionaries, decision-makers, and guides. That statement was accompanied, however, by their acceptance of and desire for the congregation to be participants in the vision, function, and future of the congregation. In other words, both the elders and the congregation would feed and provide for one another, taking ownership in the congregation's work and development.

Ethical Leadership and Followership

A comprehensive study of ethics and ethical behavior is much broader than the scope and purpose of this book. The topic is just simply too big because of the place and function of ethics in so many areas of concern, on a variety of levels. I will, therefore, make some brief observations about the function of ethical thinking in leadership and limit those observations to biblical ethics that impact the way church leaders act as servants. These ethical concerns stem directly from the elements of reciprocity and symbiosis, and the issues of trust and provision.

I mentioned in chapter one the connection made by Northouse between servant leadership and ethical leadership, and that such a connection is both intriguing and problematic. One of the more intriguing aspects of such a connection is that it demands ethical behavior from leaders, for they are servants. In other words, I insist that servant leadership naturally and necessarily implies ethical behavior, and ethical behavior naturally and necessarily implies servant leadership.

Consider the list of leadership characteristics Paul constructed in 1 Timothy 3.1–6. While some of them are concerned with moral and social conduct such as being sober-minded, self-controlled, respectable, hospitable, and not a drunkard, there are those that reflect clear, biblical, appropriate ethical choices such as being above reproach, not violent but gentle, and not a lover of money, as well as managing his house well while his children are in submission with reverence.

In Acts 20.31 Paul instructed the elders of the Ephesian church to be alert. Alert to what? They were to be alert to the threat of "fierce wolves" who would come in among them and not spare the flock (v. 29). They were also to be alert to those who speak "twisted things" ("perverse things," KJV, NKJV; "distort the truth," NIV) that they might draw away the disciples toward their false teaching (v. 30). Peter emphasized that elders are not to shepherd for "shameful gain, but eagerly" (1 Pet. 5.2).

All of this implies a strong ethical sense within the hearts and intentions of the shepherds of the Lord's church. Not only are they to be men of a moral and social outlook that is centered on biblical principles, but they are to be men who wish to always do the right thing for the good of the congregation as a whole because they are servants, too; they are servants of the Lord.

The work of ethical leaders must be focused on the people being led and the leader must be keenly aware of how his decisions will impact others. A key component of ethical leadership is accountability.[23] In this way, ethical leadership seeks to serve the greater good rather than focusing on what is self-serving. Ethical accountability demands that the leaders take responsibility for the future of the congregation. Greenleaf refers to this, in part, as foresight, which he defines as "regarding the events of the instant moment and constantly comparing them with a series of projections made in the past and the same time projecting fu-

---

[23] Bass, *Handbook*, 362.

ture events—with diminishing certainty as projected time runs out into the indefinite future…The failure (or refusal) of a leader to foresee may be viewed as an ethical failure."[24] Whether one agrees or disagrees with Greenleaf,[25] his point has some merit. Leaders, and so congregational leaders, are to be shapers of the future,[26] so one of their chief tasks is to discern, process, and understand how the organization can effectively face the challenges and opportunities of the future.

The utilization of power is an ethical concern that is connected to leading the congregation toward effective work as well as into the future. It is, in fact, an element of perhaps every concern in the study and understanding of leadership. The element of power is of specific concern in the leader-follower relationship because power is too often associated with and given to the leaders, while powerlessness is associated with and given to the followers. Ethically, leaders must be willing and able to be the source of power for their followers and to give power to them as well.

Motivating followers to put the needs or interests of the group ahead of their own is another quality of ethical leaders. Motivating involves engaging others in an intellectual and emotional commitment between leaders and followers that makes both parties equally responsible in the pursuit of a common goal. These characteristics of ethical leaders are similar to inspirational motivation, which is a style component of transformational leadership. Inspirational motivation describes leaders "who communicate high expectations to followers, inspiring them through motivation to become committed to and a part of the shared vision of the organization."[27]

---

[24] Greenleaf, *Servant Leadership*, 39.

[25] It is possible, even logical perhaps, to see Greenleaf's assessment of a lack of foresight as "ethical failure."

[26] I will discuss vision casting in chapter four.

[27] Northouse, *Leadership*, 179.

Similarly, ethical leadership intends to inspire and stimulate leaders and followers toward *visionary behavior* that is transformational and that moves the organization in a positive (ethical) direction. The term "visionary behavior" implies the actions and intentions of an organization collectively toward the fulfillment of a vision; all that is done seeks a positive outcome toward the vision and effectiveness of the organization. Ethical leaders assist followers in gaining a sense of personal competence that allows them to be self-sufficient by encouraging and empowering them, as well as forming a moral and ethical foundation for what is to be accomplished.

FOUR | *Vision Casting and Mission Statement*

Allow me to briefly mention two peripheral issues at this point, one that can be a factor in the concerns of this chapter, which are vision casting and a statement of mission. Two words, leading and managing, are significant to this discussion and are often used together. Understanding their similarities and differences can be helpful in recognizing the function of casting a vision and making a statement of mission.

Some reject leadership and management as similar in scope. Ian Fair believes that leadership is not management.[1] He differentiates the two terms by stating that "management is more focused on the control of tasks and leadership is more interested in the development of people."[2] While I agree it is a mistake to confuse leadership and management, I also believe it is a mistake to assume management has no place in the overall task of spiritual and congregational leadership. They are similar in that both involve "influence as a way to move ideas forward, and both involve working with people."[3] What does leading and management

---

[1] Ian Fair, *Leadership in the Kingdom: Sensitive Strategies for the Church in a Changing World* (Abilene, TX: ACU Press), 1996.

[2] Ibid., 119.

[3] Robert Banks and Bernice M. Ledbetter, *Reviewing Leadership: A Christian Evaluation of Current Approaches* (Grand Rapids, MI: Baker Academic,

look like in a congregational setting? The difference between the two terms is found in how they function, and considers what one is expected to do. Put simply, the act of "leading" focuses on the act of making sure the right things are done, while "management" focuses on doing things the right way.[4] According to Robert Banks and Bernice Ledbetter, "management is about coping with complexity—it is responsive" and "leadership is about coping with change—it too is responsive, but mostly it is proactive. More chaos demands more management, and more change always demands more leadership."[5]

In general, the leader is concerned with the spiritual and emotional issues of the congregation and the manager is concerned with the physical issues. The leader focuses on things such as spiritual growth and faith development, while the manager focuses on things such as budgetary concerns, communication, and "plant" maintenance. Both are essential to proper congregational leadership.

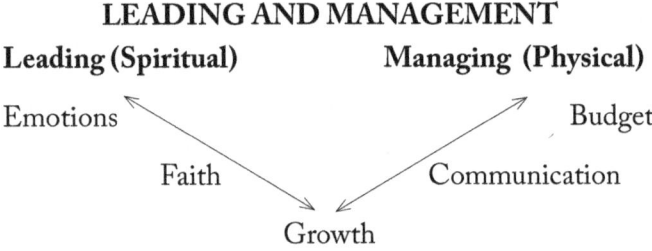

Fig. 3- Leading and Management

That is not to say a "leader" and "manager" are so simply separated in function or purpose. Like a manager, a leader is also concerned about the physical aspects of the congregation; like

---

2004), 17.

[4] Ibid.

[5] Banks and Ledbetter, *Reviewing Leadership*, 17.

Vision Casting and Mission Statement | 99

a leader, a manager is concerned about the spiritual. Each will overlap and embrace both essential aspects of the congregation. I will address this again, as well as other connected concerns in the discussion of strategy, so we will move on.

This chapter addresses primarily the key issues of vision casting and the making of a statement of mission. I will address them individually and then bring them into focus as companion tasks for all leaders and leadership.

Vision Casting

John Kotter defined "vision" as "a picture of the future with some implicit or explicit commentary on why people should strive to create that future."[6] While I believe this definition leaves the reader wanting more,[7] Kotter offers the imagery of vision being a picture of the future that requires people to implement it, which are key elements of vision.[8]

Elements of VISION
A Picture ─────> Of Future ─────> About People

Problems in leadership, organizational management, and organizational systems often arise, at least in part, due to some type of vision malfunction. That malfunction might be categorized in two ways. First, no vision has been cast nor a mission stated at all. This is too often the case with congregational lead-

---

[6] John P. Kotter, *Leading Change* (Boston, MA: Harvard Business School Press, 1996), 68.

[7] His use of the phrase "implicit or explicit commentary" is rather vague. To be fair, however, his definition possibly is intentionally stated in this way to move the reader further into his discussion, perhaps toward his information regarding clarification.

[8] I will borrow a list of key elements in the process of implementing change from Kotter in chapter seven that will repeat some of the information in this chapter. I will also omit the process of offering the congregation (organization) incremental short-term wins for this chapter and briefly discuss it in chapter six.

ership that fails to see the necessity and benefit of forward thinking and future planning; the leadership feels there is no need to do anything other than "business as usual." It is the church, not a company, and the job is spreading the Gospel, they might feel, so no planning or strategy is needed. This is often associated with congregations that favor the "ole' time religion" or "the little brown church in the vale" mentality. They are settled and set in the way things have always been done, so planning and strategy is unnecessary, they believe.

Ironically, they may not realize that harboring such traditional ideology is a form of vision casting and statement of mission, albeit a potentially ineffective form. An old song from the 1990s asserted, "If you choose not to decide you still have made a choice."[9] In other words, even if someone believes he has made no decision by choosing not to decide, in doing so he still made a choice—the choice not to decide. In a similar way, congregational leaders who choose to cast no vision or make no mission statement actually have cast a form of a vision or have made a form of mission statement; their vision is to cast no vision and their mission statement is to state none. Consider 1 Corinthians 3.6: "I planted, Apollos watered, but God gave the growth." Within this passage is a clearly stated plan of action, a vision of evangelism and a fulfillment of Matthew 28.19–20. Both Paul and Apollos had their specific tasks, to plant and then water evangelistic seed, and then be faithful enough to look for the increase that can and will only come through the power of God. It is a vision realized through their combined efforts.

Second, the vision cast and/or mission stated is unrealistic or ill-conceived. This is often the plight of churches with existing, but limited forward thinking; sometimes a vision is cast either too

---

[9] Geddy Lee, Erick Lifeson, and Neil Peart, "Freewill," *Permanent Waves* (Anthem: Canada), January 1, 1980.

low or too high. In other words, the vision either does not take into account the potential resources and opportunities available for success or it assumes more resources and potential for success than is realistically available. Vision and mission are perhaps also bogged down in budgetary concerns and find little time to think beyond the next contribution. They mean well and desire to improve, but never seem to rise above a certain criteria such as cost, prior failed attempts, or low estimations of resources.

This malfunction reveals a management-vs-leadership approach. Leadership that is visionary tends to dream bigger and broader than appearances might assume. They see past obstacles that they perceive to be surmountable. Management tends to be bottom-line oriented, driven by what they perceive rather than dream. Malfunctioning leadership and management are responsible for hundreds of congregations floundering, stumbling, and even falling, sometimes time after time. Both malfunctions stem from a misunderstanding of how the congregation functions as a fluid body. Ironically, the leadership of these congregations is usually made up of men who realize the value of forward thinking, strategy, and organizational issues. They are farmers, engineers, foremen, educators, administrators, coaches, buyers, scientists, and a host of other occupations demanding such insight, but they feel those things do not apply in regard to leading the congregation. It is the leadership, willing to both lead and manage, that must seek after the vision and mission of the congregation. In order for that to be done, congregational leaders must understand what vision is and how it is cast, and then how it is managed. I should explain at this point that leadership and management are not opposite perspectives or approaches. Earlier, I stated that the second malfunction of vision casting is an unrealistic or ill-conceived vision, and that leaders and managers respond differently. The point is not that congregational elders should be leaders and not managers, but leaders when needed and managers when needed.

The thrust of a "vision" is forward, into the future, with a specific direction in mind. "Vision," however, has not been a universally accepted term. In times past, and perhaps even today among some, secular management sectors have favored the term "purpose." Recent studies[10] have begun to elevate "vision" above "purpose," or any other term for that matter. Kouzes and Posner defend the use of "vision": "...not because it is fashionable but because it is the most descriptive term for the ability that leaders discussed with us. We prefer *vision*, first of all, because it is a "see" word. It evokes images and pictures. Visual metaphors are very common when we are talking about the long-range plans of an organization. Second, *vision* suggests a future orientation—a vision is an image of the future. Third, *vision* connotes a standard of excellence, an ideal. It implies a choice of values. Fourth, it also has the quality of uniqueness. Therefore, we define a vision as an ideal and unique image of the future."[11]

Robert Dale defines "vision" as "the power you have to see, imagine, and perceive things not yet visible and events not yet attempted."[12] John Maxwell illustrates vision casting with an example from Henry Ford:

> I will build a motorcar for the multitudes. It will be large enough for the family but small enough for the individual to run and care for. It will be constructed of the best materials, by the best men to be hired, after the simplest designs that modern engineering

---

[10] Such as W.B. Bennis and B. Nanus, *Leaders: The Strategies for Taking Charge* (New York: Harper and Row, 1985), 89, for example.

[11] Kouzes and Posner, *The Leadership Challenge*, 85.

[12] Robert D. Dale, *Pastoral Leadership: A Handbook of Resources for Effective Congregational Leadership* (Nashville: Abingdon Press, 1986), 95.

can devise. But it will be so low in price that no man making a good salary will be unable to own one—and enjoy with his family the blessings of hours of pleasure in God's great open spaces.Maxwell comments, "Henry Ford carried out that vision with the Model T, and it changed the face of twentieth-century American life.[13]

There is a "dream-like" dimension to vision and its casting must reflect that dimension. I am reminded of a series of commercials for a leading lending institution. In them a small business owner imagines (envisions) the possibilities, seeking to envision the business bigger and better by forming a frame with the thumb and forefinger of each hand and "seeing" the business with more space and more customers. So it is with casting the vision for any organization, including the organization that is the congregation. It requires the ability to see beyond present realities and envision what the organization will look like when the vision is realized. In other words, vision is faith-driven and until faith is incorporated into its casting, that vision will remain poorly formed. Spiritually, it is envisioning the congregation in a bigger building, with more people, doing things bigger and better.[14]

Consider, for example, how many goals and plans for congregations are based first and foremost on budgetary concerns. That is not to say that the budget is not to be a foundational issue in setting goals for the congregation, but there is an element of faith involved as well. I am reminded of the movie of several years ago, "Field of Dreams,"[15] and the much-quoted line, "If you build it, they will come." The element of a *leap of faith* in

---

[13] John C. Maxwell, *The 21 Irrefutable Laws of Leadership: Follow Them and People Will Follow You* (Nashville: Thomas Nelson Publishers, 1998), 121.

[14] By "bigger" and "better" I do not equate size with improvement. I am using the two terms as references to bigger and better ideas, practices, and results.

[15] Gordon Company, 4/21/89, director Phil Alden Robinson

that statement is clear and it expresses, to some extent, the faith-driven foundation that is to motivate the act of vision-casting: "If you envision it, it can happen." Faith involves a development of the future: the desire to gather the resources necessary to build a future of one's choosing.

Ideally, budgets should serve as a tool of implementation,[16] not a foundation for vision. While congregational leaders should be faithful stewards of the resources in which they are entrusted, financial resources, budgetary concerns, the so-called "bottom-line" are limited to *what is* rather than *what could be*. Leaders would be well-served to allow budgets to assist in determining where they and the congregation are in the implementation of the vision, rather than a determining factor in the validity and vitality of the vision itself.

Vision casting arises then from hope and a commitment to the future. In a way, vision-casting involves picturing what is, according to conventional wisdom, unlikely and perhaps even impossible. It is the mechanic looking intently at a rusted 1939 Ford with no seats or working engine, but envisioning a valuable, restored collector's item. It is the one who stands in an empty field filled with rocks, trees, and the trash of generations, but envisioning a recreation center for the community. It is Sam Walton standing in front of a Five-and-Dime on the town square of Bentonville, Arkansas, but seeing the international phenomenon, Walmart Corporation.

Jesus offered one of the greatest expressions of vision-casting in all of Scripture: "And I also say to you that you are Peter, and on this rock I will build My church, and the gates of Hades shall not prevail against it" *NKJV* (Mt. 16.18). This vision of Jesus is a part of the overall kingdom vision He had made so extremely clear throughout His ministry, placing it in the possession of

---

[16] I will discuss implementation in some detail later in this book.

those who are poor in spirit (Matt. 5.3), emphasizing it in His model prayer (Matt. 6.10), expressing its entrance through water and the Spirit (John 3.5), and emphasizing that it was not be of this world (John 18.36). It was a vision that began with the pronouncement of the covenant of God, the kingdom that would arise from it, and the glory of heaven that would be its fruition. The Son of God was incarnated to bring salvation to the world, preaching and teaching the message of redemption, and was then tried, crucified, and buried so that the world would realize the splendor of the resurrection. That vision, cast through the proclamation of the Gospel message, ushered the world into the realm of eternal hope. Consider also the vision statement of the Lord through the prophet Joel regarding the Spirit and the call to salvation:

> And in the last days it shall be, God declares, that I will pour out my Spirit on all flesh, and your sons and your daughters shall prophesy, and your young men shall see visions, and your old men shall dream dreams; even on my male servants and female servants in those days I will pour out my Spirit, and they shall prophesy. And I will show wonders in the heavens above and signs on the earth below, blood, and fire, and vapor of smoke; the sun shall be turned to darkness and the moon to blood, before the day of the Lord comes, the great and magnificent day. And it shall come to pass that everyone who calls upon the name of the Lord shall be saved (Joel 2.28–32; Acts 2.17–21).

Notice the use of phrases such as "it shall," "I will," "shall," and "shall come." These are good examples of vision language; it is the use of words that convey intentions, dreams, and plans. These phrases are not combined with "maybe," "might," or "perhaps."

While failure is possible and even inevitable if one jumps out far enough or moves far enough out on the proverbial limb, there is a strong intentionality to vision casting. Vision casting is done for the purpose of accomplishing what is planned, providing "a clear mental picture of how things should be, regardless of how they are now."[17] This describes one of the hardest steps to take in vision casting for any organization, including congregations: a potentially positive view of the future in spite of an unfavorable present and past.

Consider "congregation A," for example.[18] Congregation A was established more than three-quarters of a century ago in the home of a local family on Main Street. It flourished for the first several years, growing dramatically, both spiritually and numerically. During this time, the congregation bought a small building in mid-downtown and three years later added classrooms. They installed three elders and appointed four men as deacons a few months after that. By their fifteenth anniversary, they had grown to over one hundred and forty in attendance on Sunday morning and had made a powerful impact on their community.

This trend continued, growing to an attendance of over four hundred, until mid-summer in their sixty-fourth year. Several traumatic events occurred soon thereafter: the resignation of five of the nine elders, the loss of two hundred and fifty of their four hundred and thirty members, and the resignation of their pulpit minister, associate minister, and church secretary. Local and foreign missions came to a halt, the contribution decreased by more than forty percent, and the reputation of the congregation was severely damaged within the community and among other churches in the area. All of this occurred as a rolling rock turned avalanche because of bad leadership through dictatorial methods and weaknesses of the flesh within the congregation. The result

---

[17] Banks and Ledbetter, *Reviewing Leadership*, 85.

[18] Congregation A is fictitious and does not represent an existing congregation.

was a fragmented congregation dominated now by mistrust and skepticism. Three and a half years following the upheaval, the decision was made to try and move beyond their past and continue the work of the Lord in that community.

Where do the elders begin? How can they accomplish such a daunting task? Are you familiar with the motivational question, "How do you eat an elephant?" The answer is, "One bite at a time." Those elders must cast their vision of what they want to do and how they want it to look, and then begin reframing and rebuilding themselves and the congregation one step at a time. The leadership of that congregation must rise above the past and cast a vision with the intention for success. That intention for success becomes the structure of their vision for the future. That structure must consist of a steady, progressive, incremental plan to right the ship, and it all must be done according to a clearly-stated, organized plan of action. Too often, elders try to move beyond a problem by only doing one thing, which is usually what they find most threatening. Those elders must take the time to assess the problem, its sources and causes, and its effect upon the congregation, and then carry out their plan for resolution. I will discuss problems and conflict, and their resolution, later in the book.

Of course, skepticism and uncertainty can be a great deterrent to vision casting. The hopes and dreams of the future can be watered-down to a pale and tasteless consistency when the past and present become the foundation for determining the future. It is not necessarily a lack of faith but a problem with trusting any vision for fear of the past and the uncertainty of the present. So then, trust may not enter the picture, as well as renewal, hope, or commitment. No vision is cast because there is no hope for the future in which that vision resides.

Nehemiah is good example of vision casting for the future. His story, strongly connected historically and functionally to that of Ezra, was one of casting a vision for rebuilding the future of a fallen city and a people in need of renewal. When informed of the plight of his people and the crumbled condition of the city of Jerusalem and its walls, he formulated a plan. First, he prayed for God's intervening power (Neh. 1.5–11). All wise congregational leaders (and organizational leaders too, for that matter) will benefit tremendously if God is the first source of strength and formation in any action taken.

Second, Nehemiah set his vision and mission—rebuilding the city he loved—in motion before the king (Neh. 2.1–6) and implemented his vision by obtaining the necessary authority, materials, and manpower to complete the task (7–10). Notice also that he supplemented his vision by viewing the walls of the city, assessing the damage, and then formulating his plans (perhaps "reformulating" is the better term) for the completion of his task.

Fig. 4- Nehemiah's Vision Casting and Statement of Mission

Nehemiah's example expresses a key element of vision-casting and implementation: communicating the vision to those who make it happen. This is often more difficult than it appears at first, because it is easier to see it in your head rather than put into words that others will understand and embrace. Perhaps you are familiar with the statement, "It sounded good at the time." The statement reflects the formulation of something that, when verbally expressed, appeared to have merit, but when it was explained or even implemented, it did not retain its validity. Such an event might be associated with the statement of some sort of ill-formed and/or ill-stated plan when others fail to grasp the significance of what someone has said, even though it is significant to the one who stated it. It might be the telling of a humorous story that does not amuse others who hear it or recounting an exciting experience that does not excite those who witness its telling.

Consider a model of vision casting and implementation that I call the "Concentric-Circle Method." Take a look a look at Figure 5 below and notice the continual movement inward, toward the center. For example, someone (the visionary) imagines (envisions) the beginning of a ministry doing foreign missions. His idea is good, well-thought-out, and practical. He can see it happening; he can envision his congregation sending a mission team into a country to extend the message of the gospel to the people there; let's say, Tanzania.

His next task is to present his vision to those with the authority to give the vision the power to become reality; the elders, perhaps, or if the visionary is one of the elders, the other elders. Once that is done, the vision must be presented to the pool of resources necessary to put feet on the ground in the mission field: the deacons and ministry staff, as well as the office staff who will provide components such as able members of the team, those who produce necessary supplies, and write and mail letters.

The final step in putting life into the vision comes when it is presented to the congregation as a whole. This final group, which of course includes those already mentioned, also contains those who will offer the emotional and spiritual support necessary to make the vision a congregational effort, rather than the work of a smaller group within the congregation. Recall Paul's inclusion of the church in Philippi in his mission, indicating that they were partners in his global work (Phil. 1.5). When missions are understood and embraced by the congregation as a whole, the effort becomes something of which the majority takes ownership.

The vision-caster(s) must be able to communicate the dream so that others will understand, embrace, and support it. Consider the following statement: "Visionary leaders are those who have the ability to capture the imagination of followers and motivate them to realize their goals for the church and for themselves. Visionary leaders sense the hidden potential that others can bring to the corporate vision, inviting their involvement in the spiritual enterprise of the church."[19] Often this is the hardest part of vision casting, just getting things off the ground, because the vision caster(s) realizes the significance of the dream, but cannot express it adequately enough to others. Noah is another great example of vision casting and implementation (Gen. 6–7). A monumental problem arose within the population of the earth: "The Lord saw that the wickedness of man was great upon the earth and that every intention of the thoughts of his heart was only evil continually" (Gen. 6.5). God decided, "I will blot out man whom I have created from the face of the land….But Noah found favor in the eyes of the Lord" (7–8). God announced to Noah His intention to destroy all of mankind, except Noah and his family (18), and instructed him to build an ark of gopher wood, with rooms, covered inside and out with pitch, with three decks, and construct it to be approximately 450 feet long, 75 feet wide, and 45 feet high.[20] As

---

[19] Shawchuck and Heuser, *Leading the Congregation*, 149.

[20] Those approximate dimensions are based on the assumption that a cubit was equal to 18 inches.

if that task was not daunting enough, God then commanded Noah to gather the male and female of all animals, seven pairs of all clean animals and a pair of all unclean animals (7.2–3), "two and two of all flesh in which there was the breath of life" (7.15).

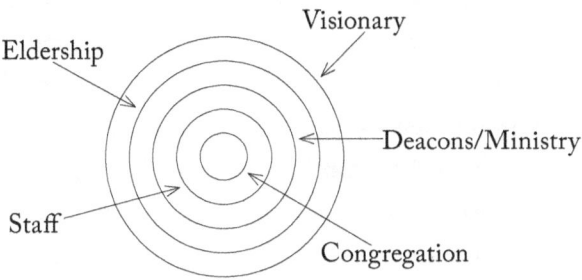

Fig. 5- The Concentric-Circle Method of Vision Casting

Wow, what a task; what a responsibility! Noah was forced to envision the ark as it would be formed and shaped, and then completed ready for his family and all of the animals to enter. He had to cut and form the wood, frame and construct the ark to accommodate the enormous volume of cargo and provisions, as well as a suitable dwelling for him and his family. How do you organize and then complete the gathering of all of those birds and animals, and then place them into their pens or cages or coops? Noah accomplished his responsibility, preserved the living creatures of God, and delivered his family through a worldwide deluge. He was given his task, developed a vision of how it would look and function, implemented that vision, and completed what God had given him to do.

A methodology must be found to enable and empower others to embrace the vision, the dream of the future. According to Israel Galindo, the key to expressing the vision so that others will understand and accept it depends on clarity.[21] **First, there must**

---

[21] Israel Galindo, *The Hidden Lives of Congregations: Discerning Church Dynamics* (Herndon, VA: The Alban Institute, 2004), 211.

be clarity of values. "You know what you value by what you practice and who you follow. What are those things that we value most?"[22] This becomes a group effort, one that occurs between the vision caster(s) and the congregation. When contemplating the common values of the congregation (not individual values alone, but the collective values of the group), it is productive to brainstorm the values that come to mind and then work through the list. As a group, that list is altered to its most efficient status. Remember, this is not a time for individuality, but collectivity. Second, there must be **clarity of identity**. This is done as a simple question: "Who are we?" This is a statement to identify who the congregation is. The statement reflects action and productivity. For example, "We are a congregation of believers who function as a family of God seeking to evangelize the community with the message of the Gospel." In that statement is the identification of the congregation, a family of God, through how it functions, evangelism. Third, there must be **clarity of choice.** The decisions of the congregation affect its future: its ministry, direction, mission, practices, commitment, and cost (spiritual and financial).[23]

All of this leads to the "what" or the "goal" aspect of vision casting and answers the question, "What will we look like when we become who we want to be?" This becomes essential in completing the vision casting process. For example, if the vision caster(s) is able to communicate effectively the dream (the "who we are"), by what method will the congregation know when they have arrived? In other words, it is all well and good to have a dream, but unless there is some goal in mind, something to identify what the dream looks like, then the vision casting will be incomplete.

Think of vision casting—who we are and what we look like—as an architectural idea. The architect has a specific structure in

---

[22] Ibid.

[23] Galindo, Hidden Lives, 211.

mind: an office complex, a hotel, or a residential dwelling. That structure is nothing more than an idea—a dream—until the blueprints are drawn and those blueprints are little more than abstract lines and shapes on special paper until an architectural model is either drawn or constructed or both. The end result is that the finished product will reflect what the architect had in mind, what was expressed in the blueprints, and what was illustrated in the model.

Elements that Encourage Volunteerism

Before I move on to the discussion of the mission statement, allow me a few moments to briefly discuss the place and function of volunteerism within the congregation.

A functional by-product of vision-casting (as well as followership) and an idea behind the concentric-circle method is volunteerism. Too many congregational leaders forget, either through a lack of knowledge or a lack of care, that those who do the work, who implement the vision and mission of the church, are volunteers. Most, if not all,,congregations have at least one paid employee, usually the preacher. Even if he works fulltime in the secular world, he is still compensated for his preaching and teaching. With each addition to the ministry staff (e.g. associate, youth, involvement, and educational ministers) and church staff (e.g. secretary, custodian), the list of paid employees increases. This number, however, represents a very small percentage of the total congregation, and that means the vast majority of those who provide the labor and physical support of the work being done are volunteers. In the majority of cases, the elders themselves are volunteers; while there are congregations that have a small percentage of elders who are paid, the majority are unpaid volunteers.

Volunteerism, as I pointed out in the field of followership, is an understudied concept within leadership, even though study has been done over the past several decades.[24] The study is even more lacking in an understanding of congregational leadership. Shawchuck and Heuser, in both of their books, *Managing the Congregation* (1996) and *Leading the Congregation* (1993), as well as Walter Wright in his book, *Relational Leadership* (2000),[25] discuss the concept and method of volunteerism from a congregational perspective. More study and application, however, must be done certainly within the discussion of congregational leadership.

From the standpoint of effective and productive leadership and followership the word "volunteer" may be unwelcome. Shawchuck and Heuser wrote, "The word *volunteer* is fraught with problems because it creates images in the minds of many that are unhealthy. Too many persons feel that if they can volunteer to do a job, they can also volunteer to do it poorly."[26] Indeed, there is truth to this assessment and not just in the secular world, but the spiritual world of the congregation as well. Leaders, secular and congregational, face the task of being leaders, and therefore taskmasters of the work to be done. If they are working with a large number of volunteers, and the congregation certainly is a good example, they face the threat of a lack of cooperation if the volunteers feel they are being manipulated, coerced, threatened, or trivialized in their efforts.[27]

So what is to be done? As with the casting of the vision and, as I will show later, the statement of a mission, those who will implement them must feel that they are an integral part of the machinery that will make it all work. Shawchuck and Heuser com-

---

[24] Kouzes and Posner, in *The Leadership Challenge*, is an example. See the bibliography for the complete reference.

[25] See the bibliography for the complete references.

[26] Shawchuck and Heuser, *Managing the Congregation*, 190.

[27] This phenomenon is seen within any number of organizations that use a large amount of volunteers: the Red Cross, a political candidate, the Salvation Army, organizations of social charity, and congregations.

mented, "Indeed, people desire leaders who can motivate them to volunteer their energies toward a collective effort. However, such leadership requires vision and the courage to lead the organization toward that realization of the vision—even when the way is uncertain."[28] Later in the book, they add, "The realization of a vision has human and relational elements to it. While spiritual energy is important for a congregation, the elements of support, trust, and open communication provide emotional and psychological energy for the entire enterprise."[29]

Trust is a key component in the placement of effective volunteers. Greenleaf wrote, "Trust is first....A serious error of an earlier generation was to put administration first. Administration is important, but it is largely a skill, and skills are secondary."[30] Servant leaders will, therefore, elicit trust, and trust must begin with the leaders giving trust to the followers who, for my point in this section, are volunteers. The giving of trust, however, is not one-directional, from leaders to followers; trust must also be given to the leaders from those who follow. Wright put it this way: "Trust is an important component of team unity. The team must trust the leader, they must know that the leader trusts them. And they must trust each other."[31]

Kouzes and Posner commented, "While substantial levels of trust may not always be required in routine work situations, trust is almost always needed when leaders are accomplishing extraordinary things in organizations. Trust makes work easier, because it forms the basis for greater openness between both individu-

---

[28] Shawchuck and Heuser, *Leading the Congregation*, 16.

[29] Ibid., 152.

[30] Greenleaf, *Servant Leadership*, 88.

[31] Walter C. Wright, *Relational Leadership: A Biblical Model for Influence and Service* (Carlisle, Cambria, UK and Waynesboro, GA: Paternoster Press, 2000), 53.

als and departments. Trust in a relationship generally develops gradually over time through the course of personal interactions."[32] It is simple, really: trust builds relationships; a lack of trust tears relationships down. Trust tends to synchronize lives, work, and visions more efficiently, especially when such trust is a result of perceived honesty and integrity.[33]

The relationship of the apostle Paul and Tychicus is a good example of the synchronization of life, work, and vision through the element of trust. Tychicus was one of Paul's companions in ministry in Macedonia and Greece, eventually waiting for the apostle and Luke in Troas (Acts 20.1–6). Paul later would trust Tychicus to declare the status of Paul and his ministry, as well as to encourage their hearts (Eph. 6.21–22; Col. 4.7–8). He also placed Onesimus, the AWOL slave of Philemon but "faithful and beloved brother," under the care and spiritual nurture of Tychicus (Col. 4.9). Paul would later also trust the church at Ephesus and perhaps Titus to the care and liaison of Tychicus (2 Tim. 4.12; Titus 3.12).

This trusting, working relationship between Paul and Tychicus allowed the apostle to do his ministry, even though he sat in a Roman prison. Wright commented, "[Paul] has no telephone or FAX machine. No e-mail. No way to communicate the details of his situation, the frustrations and the hopes, the challenges and the fears. But he has Tychicus. He has a close trusting relationship with Tychicus."[34] Trust is a key component of vision-casting and the implementation of it. Without trust, there can be no effective vision to be cast, for to do so, both leaders and followers/volunteers must be attuned to one another in thought, purpose, and heart. Without trust, there will be no statement of mission, which I will discuss later, for there can be no synchronization of

---

[32] Kouzes and Posner, *The Leadership Challenge*, 151.

[33] Wright, *Relational Leadership*, 77, 137.

[34] Ibid., 150.

purpose and action. Without trust, there can be no implementation because leaders and followers/volunteers will have no mutual basis from which to do the work.

Trust is also an essential element in the leader-follower/volunteer relationship because of its connection to effective, on-going communication. I will discuss elements of communication later, but let us make a few observations here in regard to trust. Shawchuck and Heuser wrote, "When the trust level is low, communication may easily become distorted. Feelings may be disguised and information falsified in order to protect oneself from perceived threat. This distortion can go both ways."[35] Communication will break down when leaders and followers/volunteers feel that others are not being open and forthcoming, or when each side feels the other has some sort of agenda behind what they say. That perceived lack of forthrightness is a serious issue of trust.

Such a breakdown in communication, and then trust, can emerge in any number of ways. For example, a congregation might not express enthusiasm for a program of community outreach because they perceive a lack of spiritual concern from the eldership (e.g. they feel the elders place more emphasis on paving the parking lot than evangelizing the community). On the other hand, those elders may not frequently express evangelistic visions but often propose facility upgrades because the congregation historically appears to express vocal support for paving the parking lot rather than evangelizing the community. The result of such mistrust is a stalemate of active vision-casting and implementation. Each side (the elders and the congregation) has a mistaken perception of the other because neither side is willing to effectively communicate.

While trust is often perceived as something earned—indeed it is, because trust is handed out from positive interaction—it is also

---

[35] Shawchuck and Heuser, *Leading the Congregation*, 152–153.

something that be given out of a desire for positive forward movement or a willingness to encourage positive action even though something less than positive may have previously been experienced. Let me use a sports illustration. I am an experienced and vocal arm-chair head coach in football or manager in baseball. So, I become a bit impatient when the quarterback or pitcher of my favorite team begins poorly, even allowing the other team to score due to his lack of performance. "Get him out of there," I might say to the television, usually after a very short amount of time. The head coach or the manager leaves his quarterback or pitcher in and, soon, the player begins to do well, even excel, eventually leading the team, my favorite team, to a decisive win. What happened? In part, it is an element of trust; the head coach or the manager trusts his player to settle down, work out the kinks, and eventually perform effectively. Trust is given even though the player may have performed poorly over a number of starts, but is given the opportunity to do better, even do well.

Trust within the congregation is too often subject to change when the perception of less than stellar performance—proper intentions and actions, or a lack thereof—dominates the implementation of the vision that has been cast. Leaders will not lead or envision the future; followers will not follow, nor will they volunteer. A lack of openness and forthrightness leads to suspicions of personal agendas or unsavory intentions. A vision cannot be cast within an atmosphere of distrust and a lack of communication.

The Statement of Mission: Mission of Purpose

The vision and its casting is only part of the process. The second step of the process is the determination of the mission. Along with the vision, the dream of the future, there must be the realization and implementation of that vision, and that emerges as a statement of mission. So, as vision-casting establishes the "what" or the dream, this second step establishes the "how" or the functionality. Robert Dale wrote, "A mission statement describes why the congregation exists and what it will attempt to contribute to the God movement. This precise and concise affirmation tells the church what its target is."[36] Dale's definition leaves a little to be desired, but it does offer three significant elements: "why the congregation exists," "what it will attempt to contribute," and "what its target is."

I like Wright's description of the mission statement better: "The mission statement is a concise description of your organization that identifies your primary goals and your distinctives. It answers the fundamental questions: Who are we? What do we do? What do we want to do? Maybe even, how do we do it? It is the final measure or standard against which all organizational decisions and activities are measured. It is a statement of your reason to exist."[37] While similar to Dale's definition, Wright's definition is a bit more concise, offering the "what" and the "who" as did Dale, but added not only the "how" but the organizational and practical purpose of the mission statement.

It is rather obvious that the casting of a vision and the mission statement are somewhat similar. They, indeed, express similar things, but remember that vision casting is about the "dream," the "who we are" and the "what will we do," while the mission statement is about how the dream will be met. I am not speaking of implementation at this point (that will come in chapter five, Strategy and Implementation), but about purpose and how an understanding of the congregation's purpose helps to focus on the "who" and "what" in the vision. Have you ever considered the purpose of the man or woman who plays certain percussion instruments in a concert orchestra: the cymbals, triangle, or whatever?

---

[36] Dale, *Pastoral Leadership*, 99.

[37] Wright, *Relational Leadership*, 84.

They stand in the back of the orchestra, near the kettle, bass, and snare drums, not far from the woodwinds, and wait for their turn in a musical piece. Their part in the arrangement is small, perhaps even minute, but when their time comes they lift their triangle or cymbals high and strike at the appropriate beat. I am thinking of the famous and much beloved *1812 Overture* with its powerful tones and dramatic instrumentation. Yet, there they are, standing in place, even occasionally striking their triangle or lightly sounding the cymbals; that is until the climatic ending and the dramatic striking of the cymbals in cadence with the playing of the other instruments. Even though they do not share in the significant role of the strings or woodwinds, their purpose is clear nonetheless. Without the tinkling note on the triangle or the crash of sound with the cymbals, the piece, whatever piece within which they function, is incomplete. When individuals know their purpose in the mission of the congregation, that mission statement becomes more effective and successful.[38] What is dreamed in the vision is expressed in the mission statement and clarified by the congregation's function within it. For example, if the vision of the Main Street congregation is to reach souls in Latin America with the gospel—"The Main Street Church of Christ seeks to preach and teach the message of the gospel to the lost souls in Latin America"—then its mission statement will express that in writing; what they want to do is expressed in a mission statement. It might be, "Seeking to evangelize Latin America, the Main Street Church of Christ will conduct annual evangelistic campaigns, working with the local preachers and their congregations through door-to-door personal work, one-on-one Bible studies, and classes for the congregations, and the preaching of sermons."

As Dale commented, "Basically, a mission statement puts the congregation's dream into words and ideas that can be commu-

---

[38] Ibid.

nicated to members and prospective members."[39] That statement becomes, in some ways, their commitment to their vision: "This is our vision and it will be our mission to do it." This is why vision casting and the mission statement complement one another. While they can and should be examined separately, they cannot effectively function separately. Each seeks to define the other: the vision is expressed in the mission statement and the mission statement is founded upon the vision.

Wright effectively wrote why the mission statement is important and how it helps the organization or, for the purposes of this book, why it is important to the church: first, Wright wrote that the mission statement "clarifies who we are….It is the charter or mandate around which the church or organization organizes itself"; second, "the mission statement is the final goal or standard by which all organizational decisions, all budget and staffing allocations are evaluated"; third, "the mission statement gives meaning to those who serve in the organization"; fourth, "the mission statement communicates to those outside the organization."[40] Wright's summary of the mission statement establishes a foundation for both the vision and mission, forming a view of the larger picture of what the organization wants to do and be. Wright's summary distinguishes some key concepts of the mission statement: clarifies the goal or standard, gives meaning, and communicates.

While the vision is simply put and the mission statement is clearly but briefly written, the far-reaching, broad-based implications of the vision and mission are clear. That is why leaders must be aware of the limits of the vision/mission. Let me first suggest that congregations must not envision themselves beyond what they are capable of doing, while at the same time they must

---

[39] Ibid. , 100.

[40] Ibid., 84–85.

seek to envision themselves in a way that promotes and demands spiritual growth, personal stretching, and a willingness to go beyond one's comfort zone. This is a difficult and frightening thing to do, for there is the risk of failure if the congregation envisions too high. At the same time, there is the reality of stagnation if the congregation envisions themselves below their capabilities.

For example, consider a congregation who envisions opening a school of preaching. That is a noble and potentially useful vision. The congregation, however, is less than one hundred people with limited financial and physical resources. How will they finance such an endeavor, and where will they conduct the classes and provide a library? Does their county or region of the state contain enough students, or any students at all for that matter? If not, students would have to come from a distance, so how will they be accommodated? It would appear the congregation has over-envisioned itself, trying to do more than its capability.

Second, it is a mistake to seek a vision based on the success of others. We are all familiar with the success stories that permeate our society. Whether it is the high school dropout who becomes a billionaire, the physically challenged person who wins an Olympic medal or enters the Hall of Fame, or Jared losing a hundred pounds by eating Subway sandwiches, we know, admire, and even envy those who envisioned high and succeeded. There are thousands of writers who want to write a best-seller or Pulitzer prize winner, thousands of athletes who want to be on the cover of sports magazines, thousands of actors who want to be thanking their fans, family, and "all who made this possible" at the Academy Awards, and thousands of musicians who want platinum sales and to win a Grammy. They will never make it, however, because fame and success are in limited supply and logic dictates that only a few find such success.

In the same way, congregations make the mistake of envisioning themselves as they see other congregations to be. This is unwise because they do not know the real nature of that congregation they admire. What they believe that congregation accomplishes may be far below realistic expectations and much less than they are able to do. In this day of statistics,[41] architecture,[42] and ministries[43] (actual or only existing on a list),[44] the competitive juices tend to flow easily. Congregation A wishes they could be more like congregation B or congregation C sees the success congregation D had with a certain event, so they wish to do it, too. Trying to cast a vision or state a mission based on what others are doing and their successes is a major mistake.

I have often wondered what the other congregations in Asia Minor thought of the church in Ephesus. They were known for their labor, patience, their intolerance of evil people, their testing of false apostles, their endurance, and their perseverance (Rev. 2.2–3). Deep down, however, beneath the bragging rights and statistics, Jesus knew that they had lost their first love (v. 4). How many churches are like Ephesus? They look so good on paper: nice facilities, state-of-the-art equipment, a long list of ministries, and a large ministry staff. They may, however, be riddled with conflict, spiritual apathy, and a host of other problems. One might be surprised how misleading surface impressions can cover a mul-

---

[41] Such as attendance figures, baptisms, and contribution.

[42] Such as floor plans and square footage.

[43] What exists in the present or only in the past.

[44] What I am thinking are the lists of ministries congregations will place on their websites and/or bulletin boards that really do not reflect what is actually being done. At one time they all were, but not in the present day. I am thinking of a congregation that has (or had) hanging on its primary bulletin board in the main foyer a list of twenty or more ministries associated with their work. In actuality, however, no more than ten of them were being done; the others were works of times past.

titude of less-than-impressive realities. I am thinking of a large, well-known congregation known for its modern facilities, large staff, seemingly unlimited resources, and so many other elements that too often define success. In reality, however, as one of the elders summarized it for me, all the elders ever really do is "put out fire." In other words, in spite of the tremendous, awe-inspiring, and enviable curb-appeal of the congregation, they rarely, if ever, moved beyond their numerous internal conflicts. It is a mistake to envision one's congregation in the light of another.

A third mistake is to forget that no two congregations are alike. Each has different resources, outlooks, and opportunities, so each congregation is able to find a worthwhile and effective purpose for their existence, regardless of how the numbers are crunched. For instance, there are congregations with an average attendance of fewer than one hundred and fifty that are able to accomplish numerous ministries and spiritual events that others double or even triple their size cannot do. The reason might be a more effective use of resources, opportunities, and personnel. Each congregation works differently, so the vision casting done for individual congregations will vary.

A fourth mistake is to forget that if a congregation is preaching and teaching the truth of the gospel, they are fulfilling a worthwhile purpose regardless of their numerical size and their seemingly vast resources. Stemming from vision/mission mistake number three, often a congregation will desire to mimic another not only because they feel the other congregation is spiritually successful, but because they feel they are not successful in what they try to do. This may be due to numbers below their expectations or some other misconception of what ministry is supposed to look like. Regardless, they feel inadequate because they do not look or act like another congregation. It must be remembered, however, that success, effectiveness, and adequacy is not dependent upon the status quo or some arbitrary measurement of success that supposedly applies to all. Vision casting and a mission statement do not come in one-size-fits-all, but are flexible, fluid, and adaptive. If all a congregation seeks to do is extend the gospel message through two evangelistic meetings each year, then a vision can be cast and a mission can be stated. The focus must be quality and not quantity.

We all know the story of The Tortoise and the Hare. While the Hare had quantity—he was really fast—the tortoise had quality—he was really focused. I believe that is part of the explanation of Ephesus losing their first love (Rev. 2). They had quantity, for they were doing a lot of good things, but they perhaps had little quality, for they had lost their focus.

The casting of a vision and the statement of a mission are essential for every congregation. They form connected acts of a congregation's leadership to seek a direction in which ministry will be done. It is a process that requires personal reflection, congregational assessment, and faith, a lot of faith. The leadership must remember, however, that the congregation is not dependent upon the vision and mission, but is founded upon faith in God: the vision that is cast and the mission statement are the results of such faith.

FIVE | *Strategy and Implementation*

Now that the vision has been cast and the mission statement has been written, it is time to implement what has been planned. In some ways, the step of implementation, which is a strategic concern, is merely an extension of the mission statement: the mission statement considers what will be done and the implementation/strategy considers how it will be done.

The apostle Paul addressed the issue of implementation, among others, in his first epistle to the church in Corinth:

> For just as the body is one and has many members, and all the members of the body, though many, are one body, so it is with Christ. For in one Spirit we were all baptized into one body—Jews or Greeks, slaves[a] or free—and all were made to drink of one Spirit. For the body does not consist of one member but of many. If the foot should say, "Because I am not a hand, I do not belong to the body," that would not make it any less a part of the body. And if the ear should say, "Because I am not an eye, I do not belong to the body," that would not make it any less a part of the body. If the whole body were an eye, where would be the sense of hearing? If the whole body were an ear, where would be the sense of smell? But as it is, God arranged the members in the body, each one of them, as he chose. If all were a single member, where would the body be? As it is, there are many parts,

yet one body. The eye cannot say to the hand, "I have no need of you," nor again the head to the feet, "I have no need of you." On the contrary, the parts of the body that seem to be weaker are indispensable, and on those parts of the body that we think less honorable we bestow the greater honor, and our unpresentable parts are treated with greater modesty, which our more presentable parts do not require. But God has so composed the body, giving greater honor to the part that lacked it, that there may be no division in the body, but that the members may have the same care for one another (1 Cor. 12.12–25).

How does this passage help us to understand the question of implementation? At first glance, the passage appears to be concerned more with the issues of individuality and community. Those issues, however, address a major concern of effective implementation: cooperative power. Perhaps you are familiar with the old example of breaking a thin stick, which is easily done. As the number of sticks increases and are combined, the task quickly becomes more difficult and then impossible. Within the bundle of sticks is found a sense of cooperative power; collectively they become more rigid and harder to break.

Kouzes and Posner commented, "Leaders realize that the key to doing well lies not in competition or in overcoming others but in gaining their cooperation."[1] Cooperation within organizations, and so churches, empowers those involved in a task through positive interaction and a shared stake in the future. This is especially effective in forming a long-lasting commitment to the cooperative task. Such cooperation enhances and stimulates the implementation of a given task.

When the act of "strategy" or "strategic thinking" is mentioned, two concepts perhaps come to mind: (1) the military and (2) the business or corporate world. The former, military strategy, might

---

[1] Kouzes and Posner, *The Leadership Challenges*, 138.

be the most logical and familiar of strategic thinking. Military leadership dynamics emerged, in part, from situational and Great Man leadership theory, where a *great man* rises up due to the situation (conflict; war; unrest) through sheer personality.[2] It has developed, to put it simply, as a form of transactional leadership where a clear distinction is made between superior and subordinates, and it is through that relationship that the subordinates are managed and developed.[3] It brings to mind scenes of war rooms filled with spit-and-polish military leadership gathered around a large map with symbols of the enemy and friendly forces arranged across its surface.

The latter, the business and corporate world, elicits images of boardrooms filled with men and women in expensive business suits focused on growth charts, statistical figures, and financial accounting. It emerged dynamically, like military and other leadership theories and methods, as a form of *big man* leadership,[4] and developed and evolved as a form of situational leadership where the right man, through personality, developed a means to lead an organization toward meeting the needs of a specific situation. Of course, business or corporate leadership has grown to proportions that cannot and should not be limited to this method or that dynamic. Overall, business or corporate leadership represents a form of organizational culture that is transformational, culture-building, and needs-oriented.[5]

When considering the methods of strategic thinking, however,

---

[2] Bass, *Handbook of Leadership*, 52.

[3] This summary is, by intention, extremely simplistic and under-stated. Of course, military leadership dynamics are much more complicated and multi-layered.

[4] Consider, for example, names such as Vanderbilt, Goodyear, Rockefeller, Carnegie, Westinghouse, and Ford.

[5] Once again, this summary is extremely simplistic and understated, for the dynamic is far too complex and multi-layered.

congregations and their leadership do not often come to mind. Just as in military campaigns and corporate planning, strategic thinking is an essential part of congregational vision casting and a statement of mission. Maxwell commented, "When failure isn't an option, nothing serves a person better than strategic thinking."[6] The comment applies certainly to the military and the corporate world, but it also applies to congregations as well. Strategic thinking, however, is not often associated with congregational leadership. "The only strategy we need is the Bible," some might insist. "Our strategy is simply doing evangelism," others might say. I could not agree more with these sentiments. What congregational leaders need to realize is that the Bible implies and employs strategic thinking, including the efforts of evangelism.

The strategic step is fundamental to any dream of a congregation's future. Jesus asked a question about strategic thinking: "For which of you, desiring to build a tower, does not first sit down and count the cost, whether he has enough to complete it?" (Lk. 14.28). Put simply, do not buy a fully-loaded luxury car if you cannot afford the payments or, even better perhaps, do not formulate a plan of action unless you have what it takes to see it through. Jesus' advice in Luke 14 is a simple issue of strategic thinking: what do we have to do, what must we have, and will we have the time needed to complete the task? No congregation will build a *tower* unless these things are considered. Ellen Van Velsor, Cynthia McCauley, and Marian Ruderman commented, "Strategic thinking includes the cognitive processes required for collecting, interpreting, generating, and evaluating information and ideas that shape an organization's enduring success."[7]

---

[6] John C. Maxwell, *Thinking For a Change: 11 Ways Highly Successful People Approach Life and Work* (Warner Books, 2003), 140.

[7] Van Velsor, McCauley, and Ruderman, *Handbook of Leadership Development*, 326.

An illustration of strategic thinking might be found in using a roadmap for planning a trip. The process is simple:

1. Choose a destination (people who travel usually have a destination in mind even if they do not intend to travel directly there).
2. Choose a route toward the destination. This may be as simple as an "A" to "B" approach or something a bit more circuitous—intending to stop here and then there before arriving at the destination.
3. Decide a duration (how long do we have to complete the trip and how long can we stay at any point along the way?).
4. Begin and complete the journey (recall the old saying that every journey begins with the first step).

All of the elements that go into planning (strategizing) a road trip are also found in planning and strategizing for the implementation of the vision and mission of the congregation: (1) choose a destination—where the congregation wants to be; (2) choose a route—how the congregation wants to get there; (3) decide a duration—how long to allow to reach the destination; (4) get started—do not become bogged down in taking the initial steps.

Strategic thinking is the means by which all that is needed to accomplish the task (based on the vision and mission) is realized. Strategic thinking also allows everyone to know what to do. Aubrey Malphurs comments: Leaders have more influence in situations where they can predict and determine that people are going to do. The more leaders can structure a situation so that people know what to do in the ministry and how to do it, the more influence a leader can have in that situation. The primary way to accomplish this very early in the ministry is to do strategic planning.[8]

---

[8] Aubrey Malphurs, *Being leaders: The Nature of Authentic Christian Leadership* (Grand Rapids, MI: Baker Books, 2003), 153.

Malphurs connects with an essential part of strategic planning and leadership: the removal of confusion and uncertainty which hinders the ability and desire to move forward. Using the imagery of planning a trip, imagine such an endeavor with confusion and uncertainty being the rule of the day.

For example, a destination is chosen but there is no knowledge of where it is in relation to the starting point: east, west, north, or south. In addition, there is no knowledge of the distance from the starting point to the destination. As the journey is begun, without any knowledge of location and distance, how long would it take for confusion and uncertainty to arise? How long would it take to begin to wonder if one is traveling in the right direction, how far he might be from the destination, or long it will take to finally arrive?

Such uncertainty represents an interruption in the momentum of any task. The loss of momentum is devastating to the implementation of a vision and mission. Poor planning and implementation, which reflects a lack of strategic thinking, puts up barriers to positive forward movement, which is a another way of understanding momentum. Organizations can suffer setbacks to their momentum from unexpected sources such as the destruction of facilities, the loss of a long-standing contract, or a change in ownership and leadership. Churches face the loss of momentum, as well. It can occur with the change of a beloved preacher, youth minister, or another member of the staff. It can occur with the death or departure of one or more of the elders or deacons. It can also occur with the destruction of the place of worship due to natural or man-made disaster. All of these events and more can bring the best of visions to a sudden halt.

What does this mean in the task of congregational leadership? Strategic thinking seeks to remove the unexpected, and form contingencies, fail-safes, and alternatives. The loss of momentum can stifle the best of plans and can occur in a number of ways such as personality conflicts, unexpected schedule and time-line changes, and the inevitability of change itself. I will discuss these issues later.

Overall, momentum can be lost when a lack of strategic thinking and planning causes plans to unravel and visions to be lost. I remember visiting a congregation years ago that had posted on a bulletin a list of ministries they claimed. The list was impressive and I said so to a man who stood next to me. He responded that they once did all of the ministries listed, but one thing or another caused most of them to be abandoned. Why? They failed to continue what they had started due to a lack of proper planning and strategic thinking. They had started out strong but later lost their momentum through ineffective strategic thinking.

In actuality, strategic thinking is more an aspect of management and not so much of leadership. In chapter four, I made a brief distinction between managers and leaders. The acts of managing and leading are "related systems of action, and both are necessary for organizational well-being."[9] Many organizations, including congregations, struggle because they have good leaders but poor managers, or vice-versa. Leaders and managers work in tandem with the other, forming the balance necessary for success, but forming that balance is a real challenge.

Banks and Ledbetter offer a contrast of the balance between the two. Leaders deal with change, creating it, responding to it, or leading it.[10] Leaders set a direction by collecting information and data within and outside the organization, finding patterns, relationships, and links. Leaders watch the big picture and monitor factors that affect the organization. Leaders pay attention to

---

[9] Banks and Ledbetter, *Reviewing Leadership*, 17.

[10] I will discuss congregational (organizational) change later.

indicators such as performance, growth and decline, and costs. Leaders pay attention to organizational processes such as innovation and morale. Leadership is about seeking adaptive and constructive change.

Managers encompass complexity through planning and budgeting, setting targets or goals for the future. This sort of planning seeks to produce order; management is about seeking order and stability.[11] Strategic thinking and planning is an act of leadership, but such thinking and planning is incomplete without the addition of management, for management compliments strategic direction setting.[12]

Again, how does this translate into congregational leadership? As stated earlier, organizations struggle because they have either good leaders but poor managers, or poor leaders but good managers, or both poor leaders and managers. Congregations everywhere have elders who do well in maintaining or managing the stability of set budgets, methods of checks and balances, and the systematic care of the physical issues of the congregation. At the same time, however, these managers have very little vision for the future; they fail to employ forward thinking and cannot, or perhaps will not, see beyond what is immediate. Their basis of operation is the bottom line of budgets and the comfort of systematic and repetitious procedure, rather than the unknown territory of coloring outside the lines.

There are a number of approaches to strategic thinking and planning that are legitimate and effective. In reality, no one method emerges above another, for each is effective in a significant way. In the development of these strategic methods, a terminology has emerged that is often tossed about rather loosely and haphazardly in a variety of settings. They are found in journals, periodicals,

---

[11] Banks and Ledbetter, Reviewing Leadership, 17.
[12] Ibid.

newsletters, and church bulletins, as well as in books on ministry, congregational studies, preaching, commentaries on both the Old and New Testament, and, of course, in books on secular and congregational leadership. The terminology includes the following.

Empowerment

The act of empowerment is essential to the success of implementing the vision and mission. John Maxwell points out that the experience of Henry Ford, the automotive assembly pioneer, was not all positive "and one of the reasons was that he didn't embrace of Law of Empowerment."[13] Neither Ford nor his son Henry Ford II allowed anyone else inside their vision. When someone had a new idea, constructed a prototype, or proposed a change in plans, either Ford would immediately resist. No one else was allowed to embrace the dream, so no one else felt empowered to assist in the continuation of the dream.

Empowerment, then, becomes an act of inclusion; the leadership will seek to include in the vision and mission those who will work to implement them. This is perhaps more essential within congregational dynamics than those of the corporate world, and certainly more so than in the political world. In the corporate world, there is a significant gap between the leadership or executive level and those who exist on the labor and professional levels of the organization. Examples of such separation are legion and are perhaps illustrated best by the geographic and so then, practical, separation of the corporate office complex and the organization's work centers (assembly plants, production facilities, etc.).

The gap between the executive level and those underneath it is much wider within the political world: the governor's office, its staff, and the populace of the state; the White House, Congress, state government, and so on down to the populace of the

[13] Maxwell, *21 Irrefutable Laws*, 122.

country. While citizens of the United States are given the *ideal* of greater ownership and participation in the affairs of the nation through congressional representation and constitutional freedoms, the notion of a direct connection between government and citizenry is exaggerated. Any sort of ownership and participation in the concerns and future of our nation within the population are overshadowed by agendas with a variety of titles. Do not misunderstand me, however, for we live in the greatest nation on the planet; we enjoy freedoms that no other nation provides. To assume, however, that our freedoms ensure a narrower gap between leaders and citizenry is very mistaken.

The gaps between leaders and followers in the corporate and political worlds cannot and should not exist within the spiritual world of the congregation. What benefits the congregation benefits the leadership and membership at the same time. In the organization that is the congregation, the need for empowerment, and so the inclusion by the leadership of the members of the congregation, is much greater. The local congregation is better suited for the inclusion of its members into the vision and mission because they are built upon the immediate needs and betterment of the congregation.

The act of empowerment has a direct connection to effective, strategic congregational leadership and the lack of a desire for empowerment leads, in part, to ineffectiveness and potential failure. Several types of leadership run counter to effective empowerment. One example would be congregational leadership that do not connect with their followers, even considering themselves above their followers, whether intentionally or through some misunderstanding of their function as leaders. I can recall an elder many years ago who expressed this sort of leadership within the congregation, even toward the other elders. His military background, in part, led him to style himself as a leader with few equals, as well as one who would not be questioned. Peter demanded that elders not be "domineering over those in your charge" (1 Pet. 5.3), yet examples to the contrary are all too evident.

Another example of congregational leadership that diminishes empowerment is one that tends to micromanage rather than delegate.[14] While others probably can be cited, two reasons for micromanagement is the elders (1) are suspicious of those who are not elders and (2) hold a desire for dominance. Such suspicion and desire for dominance might emerge when the eldership seeks to hoard information and, so then, power. Since empowerment requires the sharing of information and control, the tendencies of this ineffective methodology are obvious; empowerment is, of course, impossible because such leadership methodology cannot dominate if those under them are given any level of inclusion into what they rigidly control.

Sadly, such dominance within an eldership is all too common. The majority of elders who do this have very benign, even courageous, intentions. They believe that as the elders, they are to shoulder the cares and concerns of the congregation, which is to a limited extent true, especially sharing sensitive information within the congregation as a whole. As shepherds, they do have the care and discipline of the congregation in their hands. Yet, to hoard information and dominate are unnecessary, for sharing can be informative and beneficial with the preacher/ministry staff—those who might have specific training and/or insights in such matters. One preacher lamented to me that the elders where he had once served refused to allow new ideas, new blood, or new power sources, as well as any sort of freedom to work within the congregation. Such suspicion and dominance often emerge from a lack of trust, a desire for exclusivity, or both.

---

[14] I will discuss delegation later.

A final example of a lack of empowerment I will mention is a tendency for the elders to feel powerless and lacking in confidence, doing little more than only maintaining what is already in place—very often only the physical plant—and seeking no development or improvement. To empower others would first mean the leadership would need to feel empowered, and such leadership feels anything but empowered. This sort of poor leadership seems to manifest itself when the elders are *burnt out* and weary of the pressures and concerns of leadership. A preaching friend of mine once confided that he believed his elders were more attuned to paying the bills and maintaining the facilities rather than evangelizing the community and spiritually nurturing the congregation. It also might manifest itself when significant decisions must be made, such as in a preacher transition. Someone once lamented to me during his own transition period, "When did elders become too frightened to lead?" Empowerment is difficult to cultivate when the leaders feel little or no empowerment themselves.

The act of empowerment carries within it the intention of allowing the congregation to embrace the vision and mission, to feel they are a part of what those in leadership have planned. Teamwork becomes a motivator for greater initiative, and that becomes a component for congregational success. Empowerment, however, is not something that is simply *given*; it must be developed between leaders and followers. For example, if an eldership casts a vision of being a missional congregation, sending teams from the congregation into the foreign mission field, empowerment[15] would become not only the acceptance and desire to take ownership in the vision, but giving the teams the means by which they can accomplish the task; to empower them to be able to realize the vision.

Jones reminds his readers that empowerment is the act of ensuring "self-leadership by giving power away so that others can

---

[15] This would also include equipping, which I will discuss later.

act."[16] This is an essential element of leadership that develops other leaders within the church. Unlike one or two of the negative examples of leadership that diminishes empowerment, effective servant leaders seek to raise future leaders from within the congregation. Maxwell's informative book, *Developing the Leaders Around You: How to Help Others Reach Their Full Potential*, begins with the author's relating the night he saw an advertisement on the back of a popular sports magazine "that caught my eye and got my emotional juices flowing."[17] It focused on John Wooden, the late coach of UCLA basketball, and the caption read, "The guy who puts the ball through the hoop has ten hands."[18] The book then emerges as a study of how to raise, create, identify, nurture, equip, develop, and form potential leaders.

The Bible addresses the development of future leaders. Paul's relationship with his younger friend and brother, Timothy, reflected the apostle's desire to develop Timothy into a leader. Paul's first epistle to Timothy certainly addressed concerns and needs of the church in Ephesus, but along the way, Paul occasionally tossed out a word of encouragement: "If you put these things before the brothers, you will be a good servant of Christ Jesus" (4.6); "But as for you, O man of God, flee these things…Fight the good fight of faith" (6.11, 12). In his second epistle to Timothy, Paul challenged Timothy to "fan into flame the gift of God" (1.6) and to "continue in what you have learned and have firmly believed" (3.14). While concerned for the future of the church in Ephesus, Paul was also concerned for the future of Timothy as a preacher and leader.

Wright refers to *empowering leadership* as "one person using his or her position…to serve and nurture another; one person see-

---

[16] Jones, *Heart, Mind, and Strength*, 120.

[17] John Maxwell, *Developing the Leaders Around You: How to Help Others Reach Their Full Potential* (Nashville: Thomas Nelson Publishers, 1995), 1.

[18] Ibid.

ing in another the potential to be more than is visible today and committing him- or herself to the development of that potential." Wright then adds, "This is what servant leadership is all about."[19] So, as I have demonstrated thus far, servant leadership is about the biblical model of being a leader to followers, the task of vision-casting and the statement of mission, and now the act of empowerment as a tool of implementation.

Jesus engaged in empowerment throughout His ministry. The "Sermon on the Mount" is a good example. In the Beatitudes, Jesus wanted the people to know that the poor in spirit would receive the kingdom, those who mourn would be comforted, the meek would inherit the earth, those who hunger and thirst would be satisfied, the merciful would receive mercy, the pure in heart would see God, the peacemakers would be called the sons of God, and the persecuted would receive the kingdom (Mt. 5). Notice, however, what He says next. He turned the audiences' world upside down by insisting that they, not the scribes or Pharisees, were the salt of the earth and the light of the world. Jesus empowered them in a way like never before (Mt. 5.3–16).

I believe the New Testament cries aloud that Jesus' use of empowerment as seen in the success of twelve individual men named to be apostles and more than one hundred additional disciples was due, first, to the ability of Jesus to complete the spiritual task He had been given by His Father. In John 17.4, Jesus prayed, "Father, the hour has come; glorify your Son that the Son may glorify you, since you have given him authority over all flesh, to give eternal life to all whom you have given him. And this is eternal life, that they know you the only true God, and Jesus Christ whom you have sent. I glorified you on earth, having accomplished the work that you gave me to do." At the age of twelve, Jesus' parents frantically searched for Him in Jerusalem when He did not return

---

[19] Wright, *Relational Leadership*, 43–44.

with them after Passover. When they found Him in the temple, He replied, "Did you not know that I must be in my Father's house?" (Luke 2.49).[20] As Jesus approached the culmination of His mission, He announced, "The hour has come for the Son of Man to be glorified," and then added, "Now my soul is troubled. And what shall I say? 'Father, save Me from this hour?' But for this purpose I have come to this hour. Father, glorify Your name" (John 12.23, 27). Everything Jesus did throughout His ministry was in regard to the completion of His mission.

Second, Jesus' success in empowering his disciples is found in three leadership components: (1) Jesus' ability to cast the vision: the kingdom of God; (2) Jesus' ability to proclaim the mission, go into the world and make disciples of the nations (Mt. 28.19); (3) Jesus' ability to empower the disciples, who in turn empowered those who would hear their message of hope. I want to examine each of these in turn, for they are essential elements in understanding how empowerment was a key component in Jesus' exemplary leadership.

- The first component, Jesus' ability to cast the vision, which is the kingdom of God, is a foundational element of Jesus' preparation of His disciples for ministry in the church of the New Testament.[21] It is found in His challenge to seek the kingdom first, before anything in this world (Mt. 6.33) or His Kingdom parables such as, "The kingdom of heaven may be compared to a man who sowed good seed in his field..." (Mt. 13.24) or, "What is the kingdom of God like?...It is like a grain of mustard seed..." (Luke

---

[20] Some translations render "in my Father's house" as "about my Father's business."

[21] The term "church of the New Testament" is intended to indicate what Jesus built upon the firm foundation of his own divinity (cf. Matt. 16.18) and how He expected the church to remain true to His vision.

13.18, 19). Through His instruction, the kingdom became something knowable and reachable.

- The second component, Jesus' ability to proclaim the mission to go into the world and make disciples of the nations (Matt. 28.19), gave the disciples a direction in which to go. He sent them out with instructions to "the lost sheep of the house of Israel" and what they can expect along the way (Mt. 10.9–33). He promised them that "the harvest is plentiful, but the laborers are few," warning them who are being sent out as "lambs in the midst of wolves" and who will be received by some but rejected by others (Luke 10.1–12). With all that He said to prepare them for the mission ahead, He promised them that He would be with them to very end of the age (Mt. 28.20).
- The third component, Jesus' ability to empower the disciples, who in turn empowered those who would hear their message of hope, suggests a successive and exponential inclusion of the generations to come. Indeed, the New Testament indicates this, for as the disciples of Jesus went out and made disciples of the nations (cf. Mt. 28.18–19), they in turn prepared those disciples for ministry and evangelism. Barnabas mentored and accompanied the persecutor Saul, who would become the apostle Paul (cf. Acts 9, 13); Paul associated with Aquila and Priscilla, and they would later teach Apollos "the way of God more accurately" (Acts 18.1, 4, 24–26). The word was preached, souls were added to the church, and more and more disciples were empowered to carry the commission of the Lord (cf. Mt. 28.18–19).

Jesus' ability to empower His disciples is seen in variety of sources. I have already mentioned His words in the Sermon on the Mount and how He insisted that they, the multitude, were the salt of the earth and the light of the world (Mt. 5.13–16). At one of Peter's most vulnerable moments, Jesus insisted that Peter would fail Him because "Satan has asked for you, that he may sift you as wheat" (Lk. 22.31). Yet, Jesus does not offer only ominous statements, but encourages Peter by saying, "But I have prayed for you, that your faith should not fail; and when you have returned to Me, strengthen your brethren" (v. 32).

In summary of this point, Jesus' ministry was not only carried out in His preaching and teaching to the multitudes, but through His preparation, the empowerment of His disciples for the coming of the church and their ministry within it. He guided them, rebuked them, instructed them, and warned them of danger. The result was an ever-growing legion of disciples who spread the borders of the kingdom of God through faithful and dedicated proclamation of the word of God throughout the known world. He commissioned them to go into the world and make disciples of the nations by baptizing them into the name of Father, the Son, and the Holy Spirit (Mt. 28.19), and that is what they did: Peter and John faced the Sanhedrin (Acts 3–4), Paul was persecuted in a variety of ways (2 Cor. 11), John was eventually exiled to the Island of Patmos (Rev. 1), and the New Testament describes others who faced danger, threat, and even death for their proclamation of the truth. They had been empowered to carry the Gospel into the world.

Equipping

The act of equipping is doing what the word implies, giving people what they need (equipment) to complete their role within the vision and mission of the congregation. Paul wrote of equipping in Eph. 4.11–13, "And He Himself gave some to be apostles, some prophets, some evangelists, and some pastors and teachers, for the equipping of the saints ("to prepare God's people," NIV) for the work of ministry, for the edifying of the body of Christ, till we all come to the unity of the faith and the knowledge of the Son of God, to a perfect man, to the measure of the stature of the fullness of Christ." Paul insists that equipping becomes the act of assignment ("He Himself gave some to be…") and then preparing them for their task ("…for the work of ministry, for the edifying of the body of Christ…"). Yet, he adds something else often overlooked in the incorporation of the vision and mission as the foundation of equipping: "till we all come to the unity of the faith and the knowledge of the Son of God, to a perfect man, to the measure of the stature of the fullness of Christ." Paul insists such spiritual equipping is for the sake of spiritual unity and knowledge so those who are so equipped will gain the fullness of Christ.

Jesus not only empowered His disciples to carry out the task of proclaiming the Gospel to the world, but He also equipped them to carry out that task. Consider, for example, the final statement of Jesus to the disciples before His ascension: "Go therefore and makes disciples of all the nations, baptizing them into the name of the Father and of the Son and of the Holy Spirit, teaching them to observe all things that I have commanded you; and lo, I am with you always, even to the end of the age. Amen (Mt. 28.19–20)." In that commission is found His empowerment of the disciples—"Go therefore and make disciples of the nations." Also contained in His statement as well is their equipping; to make disciples of the nations, He gave them the means to do so:

1. Baptism in the name of the father, Son, and Spirit
2. Teaching them to observe (obey) His commands
3. The assurance of His presence with them until the end of the age

Jesus made sure His disciples were properly prepared for their task by giving them the power to embrace the vision and mission as their own—evangelism—and by making sure they had been properly provisioned for their work.

Too often, equipping or preparation for the task is inadequate, and that will force a change in the vision and mission. In other words, leaders will sometimes allow the act of preparation and equipping to drive what the vision and mission will become. For example, imagine a congregation who envisions themselves as a community mission-oriented congregation. So, they develop a mission statement that utilizes a three-step plan to evangelize door-to-door. If, however, their preparation to carry out this vision and mission is inadequate—i.e., they do not have the resources necessary to carry out their proposed mission—the reality of their situation will alter their vision and mission in some way. So then, if the preparation is inadequate, they will have to change the plan (the vision). In this way, their lack of equipping of those who will implement the vision and mission forces changes in plans. Congregational leaders, as well as secular leaders, must actively and responsibly engage in equipping the flock, giving people what they need to complete their role within the vision and mission of the congregation.

Assessment

The process and task of assessment is vital to fulfilling the vision and mission of any organization, including—perhaps particularly—a congregation. The idea of assessment is a part of leadership from a variety of perspectives: perception, appraisal, discernment, and so on. In many books on the subject, assessment is not discussed beyond a mention here and there. In their informative book, *Managing the Congregation*, Shawchuck and Heuser offered a brief statement that placed assessment within partnership structures where the task of assessment is associated with supervision and performance appraisal.[22] Van Velsor, McCauley, and Ruderman spent much more space in discussing assessment, placing it within the tasks of coaching, development, feedback-intensive programs, and strategic thinking: "Leader development begins with assessment."[23] Rochelle Melander also places assessment within the task of strategy, or at least that assessment must be done strategically, offering thoughts on personal assessment, situational assessment, purpose, and how all of these things might be combined to produce more effective strategic leadership.[24]

For my purposes, I believe assessment is the ability to see things and people as they really are, whether that reality is positive or negative. This definition is not intended to be in contrast to casting a vision (seeing things as they can be), for assessment is a tool by which the vision is realized. Assessment is the ability to see the present—the here and now—that too often is modified for unrealistic purposes, such as convincing oneself that the congregation is greater and its resources are better than they really are at that time. This may be a problem with congregations who have had rather successful pasts filled with dynamic evangelistic, educational, and worship programs. They might tend to rationalize those same dynamics in the present, even though such success and prosperity no longer exist.

Effective assessment emerges from the ability to properly discern (assess) what is really going on within the congregation and what resources (human and material) are really available. The ability to see the situation for what it is can make or break a congregation or organization. Unrealistic assessments can under- or overestimate the potential and abilities of a congregation. The result is

---

[22] Shawchuck and Heuser, *Managing the Congregation*, 190–191.

[23] Velsor, McCauley, and Ruderman, *Handbook*, 328.

[24] Rochelle Melander, *A Generous Presence: Spiritual Leadership and the Art of Coaching* (Herndon, VA: The Alban Institute, 2006), 190–195.

a congregation that never seems to live up to its potential, so soon the potential is lost, or a congregation that accomplishes little of its vision and mission because it is not capable of completing the task.[25] Jesus offered a wonderful example of proper assessment in His ministry by taking twelve men of diverse backgrounds, experiences, and talents and turning them into apostles. For example, Jesus was able to look beyond the rough exterior of the fisherman-turned-fisher-of-men and see Peter the Gospel proclaimer (Acts 2) and pillar of the church (Gal. 2.9). Consider also the example of Saul-turned-Paul, the apostle of missionary journeys across the known world. Jesus was able to look beyond the persecutor (Acts 8.1; 9.1–2) and see the man who would fight a good fight, finish the race, and keep the faith (2 Tim. 4.7).

Let us return to the example of Peter once again. Luke's gospel records a remarkable experience shared between Jesus and Peter during the Last Supper and just prior to Jesus' arrest, trial, and then His death, burial, and resurrection. On the heels of the discussion among the disciples about who would be the greatest in the kingdom, Jesus spoke to Peter directly and said, "Simon, Simon, behold, Satan demanded to have you, that he might sift you like wheat, but I have prayed for you that your faith may not fail. And when you have turned again, strengthen your brothers" (Luke 22.31–32). Just imagine being a fly on the wall during that statement to the apostle! Peter, perhaps incredulous and certainly not understanding the thrust of Jesus' statement, replied, "Lord, I am ready to go with you both to prison and to death" (33), to which Jesus dropped the bombshell, "I tell you, Peter, the rooster will not crow this day, until you deny three times that you know me" (34). In spite of Peter's prior rashness, immaturity, lack of proper faith, and so on, Jesus was able to assess the apostle for whom he really was. Jesus knew that Peter was much more than

---

[25] See "Resources/Counting the Cost" later.

the one who, at that moment, would deny even knowing Him. I am convinced that Peter had no intention whatsoever to deny his Lord—he loved Him far too much—but Jesus knew what really lay within the heart of His disciples, at that moment in time. Jesus also knew, however, the potential that lay within Peter that, if allowed to flourish, would strengthen the hearts and lives of the church. Jesus is by far the best example of assessment the world has ever and will ever see.

It is in this way that assessment carries within it the ability to see the potential in others, as well as the congregation as a whole. Consider for a moment the example of a little league baseball coach. He has before him a collection of young would-be athletes who want to play the sport. Of course, there are plenty who want to pitch and others who desire to play one of the bases, while few desire to play in the outfield, especially right field, that proverbial land of exile where the least talented are assigned. Yet, all of the positions need to be filled and each position is important to the team. It is important for that coach to gather his young, eager players and assess them for their individual talents and abilities to contribute to the team. While several of them want to pitch, very few can, so the coach must be able to see the talents of the others and place them where they can best produce. While several of them want to play first base or shortstop, very few can, so the coach must place the others where they will be able to develop as baseball players and as contributing members of the team. Perhaps one or two have few talents in the field, but have the ability to hit or their prowess with the bat is lacking, but they have some ability to field the ball. Either way, the coach's assessment of their proper place on the team will contribute to their own physical and emotional development as members of the team and the team's ability to do well throughout the season.

So it is within the congregation. Its leadership must be able to see where specific talents lie and utilize them in the most effective way. In this way, assessment is a key element of strategic thinking. Consider what assessment is in military planning. Battles are literally won and lost due to the type of assessment done: the ability or lack thereof to look upon the enemy forces, the battlefield, and the conditions of the day and assess what it will take to be successful. In fact, in every level of competition (battle included), assessment is key to winning. In the same way, congregational leaders must be able to look on the task ahead, observe the circumstances surrounding the task, and assess what is needed for success.

It is not just a consideration of who *will* teach in the educational programs, but who *can* teach; who *can* be trained and motivated to do so effectively? The leadership must look among their young men and see potential elders and deacons to take the work of the congregation effectively into the future. It is not just those who always bring their Bibles and materials to class, who volunteer for duties within the congregation, or who appear to be more spiritually-minded. Proper assessment is also the ability to see the potential lying just beneath the surface.

I am thinking of a wonderful older couple in a congregation in north central Indiana who took the time to encourage and motivate the immature and uncertain youngest son of its preacher. They saw potential in this young man as a preacher and teacher, so they offered encouragement, constructive criticism, the occasional push, and constant love. He grew spiritually, physically, emotionally, and academically, and has now been preaching for thirty-eight years and is the author of this book. Their assessment of me was a motivating factor of what I have become.

Assessment of potential in others and the reality of a situation are both essential and beneficial to congregational leadership.

This assessment allows for proper, effective empowerment and equipping, and addresses potential, eliciting the very best from all who are involved. It is knowing the inexperienced youth in Jeremiah but seeing the prophet (Jer. 1.6–10).It is recognizing the unclean lips of Isaiah but seeing the prophet (Is. 6.5–10). It is seeing the potential preacher, teacher, song leader, prayer leader, youth leader, organizer, and manager within the membership of the congregation and developing their potential. It is the act of training, motivating, and guiding those individuals toward effective work within the congregation.

Perhaps you have heard the story of Michelangelo and his preparation to sculpt the statue of David. He and his assistant traveled to the marble quarries to choose a slab of marble for the task. While his assistant pointed out potential slabs from time-to-time, Michelangelo continued to wait for the right one. Finally, seeing a slab of the stone nearby, he proclaimed he had found what he needed. Perplexed, the assistant wondered what made that slab of marble better than the others. "Because I see the man in the marble," proclaimed Michelangelo. Such is the task of assessment and congregational leaders must do it.

Assimilation

I will only briefly discuss the topic and concern of assimilation. The thrust of this section is to offer the challenge to properly assimilate as a part of the larger concerns of strategy and implementation.

The ability to bring new faces and talents into the unfolding of the vision and mission of the congregation is essential to the success of the task ahead. A simple example is the "new family in the church" phenomenon we are all aware of. The congregation has its rhythms, ideologies, procedures, and customs, but when the "new family" arrives, everything begins to change, even just a bit. Everyone might be thrown off their rhythm and lose their momentum because a group of new people have arrived who do not know how things are done. This does not have to be the case and should not be the case if a congregation seeks to implement its vision and mission effectively. As we will see later, assimilation is a facet of the larger issue of change, and change can be frightening and intimidating. Assimilation requires adding new faces, talents, and perspectives into the mix. That takes some effort and carries with it the potential for conflict, which I will discuss in chapter six.

My wife and I spent several years as house parents in Christian childcare (for teen age boys in Indiana and teenage girls in South Carolina). One of the conflicts that would arise was when a new boy or girl would come into our house. We had spent some time organizing the house with the children we had, setting schedules and learning routines. Then, a new child would arrive, frightened and angry and confused, and he or she had to be assimilated into the family. Never was it flawless and seamless, rarely was it easy, but mostly it was successful. It had to be done or we would fail to serve the child placed into our care.

Congregations across the nation go through the "revolving-door" syndrome—the come-and-go phenomenon of gaining and losing members—especially if they exist in a community where there are several congregations in a relatively small area. A new family or two places their membership within a given congregation, but over a period of time they feel unused or even unappreciated—unassimilated—so they leave that congregation and attend another. New members and talents must be assimilated into the congregation and its work, or new members and talents will be lost.

Assimilation becomes an issue of inclusion and acceptance, but to indicate assimilation is simply inclusion might be a bit misleading, perhaps even incorrect. While the task of inclusion appears to be a tool of empowerment, it is at the same time a tool of assimilation. Inclusion through empowerment is the willingness and ability to include the congregation in the vision and mission, to embrace what the congregation will do and become. Inclusion through assimilation seeks do something similar—embrace the work and development of the congregation as one of its own—but assimilation is not the act of empowering new members. Rather, it is the act of absorbing and blending new members into the flow and patterns of the congregation.

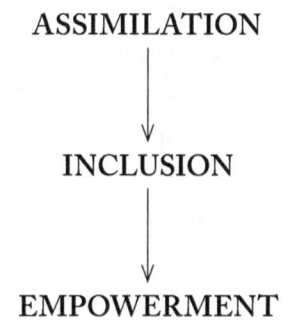

While the acts of empowerment and assimilation overlap in some ways, they are actually two different efforts of leadership. The leaders of the congregation must recognize this and make every effort to allow its members to feel included and accepted. Of course, this is never completely possible, for every congregation has its share of those who remain on the "fringe," failing to take part in or take advantage of the activities and plans of the congregation. Regardless of what is accomplished, they remain outside of the fellowship and participatory elements of the congregation. So they are never really assimilated into the congregation. They are faces in the assembly or names on a mailing list; in a way, wispy presences that merely come and go with little contact with others.

There is no best way to assimilate new or returning members into the ebb and flow of the congregation. Methodologies and ideologies abound; some of them have been proven to be effective, at least to some extent, but others have become little more than futile efforts. Why is assimilation so difficult and too often ineffective? Spiritual and congregational leaders must realize the importance of assimilation as a strategy for success in leadership. The reality is, however, that too many congregations face obstacles to assimilation, as well as a number of other programs of work and improvement. This is an unfortunate reality within contemporary congregational life and arises for a number of reasons.

Consider two of those reasons. First, the often-cited "postmodern" thinking in contemporary society. Postmodernism is categorized as a self-centered, skeptical, and apathetic time in our society's history, and such attitudes do not lend themselves to participation in group activities and the collective efforts of the congregation. Such is considered, perhaps, to be restrictive and limiting to those who see themselves and their own needs as primary. Second, the loss of "family" within contemporary congregations has taken its toll. "Back in the day," one's congregation was the spiritual family in more than the ideals of preaching, the reading of scripture, and congregational worship. Weekly activities were often centered to some extent on the activities of the congregation. This is by no means the case today, where one's modern schedules seem to take precedence over any sort of church activity.

Churches benefit from effective efforts of assimilation. Inclusion and acceptance are indeed major components, but concepts such as allegiance, spiritual family, spiritual body, cooperation, communication, and relationship are also essential. While no methodology emerges as best, the effort to assimilate is paramount. Leaders must seek to assimilate all who are new to the congregation.

Resources/Counting The Cost

Congregational leaders must be aware of the importance of gathering and using the resources available to them, making sure there are enough resources to handle the responsibilities and costs (financial and otherwise) of the vision and mission. The leadership must ask the question, "Do we have what is needed to bring this vision and mission into reality?" George Barna comments, "The expression 'anything good is worth paying for' is certainly true of God's vision for your ministry. And make no mistake about it; you will pay a price for your commitment to the vision."[26]

Consider the example of merchandizing and the statement, "You get what you pay for." In other words, there is a big difference between genuine leather and an imitation of it. I recently bought a radio/CD player for what I believed to be a very good price. I brought it to my office, plugged it in, and inserted a CD of some of my favorite music. The CD played well and the speakers produced a good sound. That is, until a few days later when the CDs began to skip and the speakers began to crackle. Yes, you do indeed get what you pay for, and if you want something of quality, you will usually pay a heftier price. Barna's caveat, "And make no mistake about it; you will pay a price for your commitment to the vision," is true. Worthwhile endeavors will require the expenditure of time, effort, sweat, and possibly some blood and tears, as well. Before congregational leaders form a vision for the church, it is imperative that that they consider the cost of reaching it.

Consider another caveat: "Be careful what you ask for. You just might get it." This statement implies a lack of understanding of the end result of the vision. After all of the time, all of the effort, and all of the stress and strain, the congregation finally has what it wanted. Sadly, they may also have discovered that they do not

---

[26] George Barna, *The Power of Vision: Discover and Apply God's Vision for Your Ministry* (Ventura, CA: Regal, 2003), 134.

know what to do with it or how to maintain it. It is vital that leaders cast a vision that can be supported, sustained, and developed with the resources they have available.

On Observatory Hill in Edinburgh, Scotland can be seen what appears to be the remains of a Greek colonnade (See Fig. 5). In reality, the columned structure, nicknamed "Edinburgh's Folly," was an attempt in the early nineteenth century to build a replica of the Parthenon in Athens in recognition of Edinburgh's reputation of being the "Athens of the North," due to the many hills upon which the city is built. The replica remains unfinished, perhaps because the city fathers did not count the cost of building such a structure. While their vision was ambitious, even admirable, their determination of available resources and cost of implementation was less so. The determination of available resources and the cost of implementation is essential to effective congregational leadership. Earlier, in some preliminary remarks about strategic thinking, I mentioned Jesus' question in Luke 14.28–30: "For which of you, intending to build a tower, does not sit down first and count the cost, whether he has enough to finish it—lest, after he has laid the foundation, and is not able to finish it, all who see it begin to mock him, saying, 'This man began to build and was not able to finish.'" Perhaps if the city fathers of Edinburgh had taken Jesus' question seriously, the construction of a replica of the Parthenon would be fact and not folly. In the same way, if the leadership of a congregation would take Jesus' question seriously, the plans and intentions of their ministry and future would be fact and not folly; a reality instead of wishful thinking.

In strategic thinking and implementation, financial resources are an essential and an oft-discussed and often controversial issue. The so-called bottom line is frequently the primary determination of a congregation's ability to carry out what is planned. "How much will it cost?" is a common question in elders' meetings and planning sessions in congregations around the country. If the leadership of a congregation will be good stewards of its financial resources, then that bottom line will take its proper and necessary place in the planning of that congregation's ministry. I fully recognize the autonomous nature of each congregation's leadership, so it is not my place, nor the purpose of this book, to overstep the authority and autonomy of any eldership. I will, however, encourage them to recall being good stewards is both responsible frugality and aggressive planning.

While it is one thing to be sure the "church's money" is being spent wisely and scripturally, it is also another thing to do little or nothing for fear of making a mistake. Elderships must find the balance between miserliness and recklessness. They will make financial mistakes, spending when saving would have been better and saving when money should have been spent. There are times when elderships must "take the plunge" or "go out on a limb," while there are times when caution is best. "When" and "how" are the tough questions, and they may or may not have clear answers. Leaders must realize that mistakes are inevitable, and knowing and embracing that will shape the decisions of leaders of faith and stewardship.

Elderships must also not make the mistake of only being concerned about *financial* resources, and not the wise, efficient, and effective use of the *human* resources within their congregation. Every congregation, regardless of size and location, has a variety of people within its membership. There are teachers, engineers, salesmen, medical personnel, executives, insurance agents, firemen, coaches, counselors, administrators, and so on. How might those people with those talents be used effectively in the strategy of implementing the vision and mission of the congregation? That becomes a task of the congregation's leadership.

How can the human resources of the congregation be used effectively? First, the leadership will want to determine what those resources are. As I mentioned above, there are a variety of professions within a congregation. The leadership must list them and use that list as a way to match a task with a resource. For example, perhaps there is a member of the congregation is who an administrator. Through his training and experience, he can be an asset when certain parts of the vision and mission must be planned, coordinated, and carried out. Perhaps a member of the congregation is an elementary school teacher. Imagine the impact of such a person if a component of the vision and mission is the revitalization of the church's educational program. Perhaps a member of the congregation is a construction company owner or construction foreman. He can be essential to the additions and changes to the church's facilities necessary in the implementation of its vision and mission. Of course, many more examples could be given, but I believe these make the point. Everyone has a talent, an expertise, or connections. The leaders will do well to tap into such resources.

Second, the eldership must organize the list into categories: leaders, followers, builders, organizers, and so on. Assign tasks to those who can and will carry them out. This point may appear at first glance to be similar or even identical to the one just made. They are, however, different. While it is important to know an individual, through training or experience, might have the ability to complete a task, but does he or she have the time?

For example, someone may be a leader, innovator, and decision-maker for a certain company, but may spend a large amount of time out-of-town, so would be unavailable to carry out a given task. Someone may be trained to carry out certain essential tasks in the congregation's plans, but may be unable to devote the time necessary due to the responsibilities of small children, elderly parents, or some similar deterrent. It is one thing to have the necessary talents and expertise at one's disposal, but that resource is rendered nil if little or no time can be spent on the task.

Knowing the human resources of a congregation is essential to implementing a strategy for completing what is planned. Congregational leaders should spend time assessing those resources and then effectively utilize them. The task of strategic thinking and implementation can be daunting, but it is essential to carrying out the vision and mission of the congregation. The tools of empowerment, equipping, assessment, assimilation, and the determination of resources and costs allow the leaders of the congregation to effectively implement their vision and mission.

SIX | *The Reality and Challenge of Change*

There is perhaps nothing more common but more frightening than the reality and even the necessity of change. Recall the illustration used earlier about the placement of a new child into our cottage at the children's home in Indiana and South Carolina. The issue was one of assimilation, even empowerment, but the biggest challenge was change; when a new child came into the cottage, there was a change in routine and in the stability we had gained prior to the child's arrival.

Change can be daunting, unwelcome, frightening, and certainly challenging, because it forces us to move out of our comfort zones, well beyond pre-established boundaries. I often use the phrase "coloring outside the lines" to describe doing what we normally would not choose to do, even if doing so would be an improvement and/or a worthy attempt. Change moves us off the plateau where we wish to make our camp, where we feel some accomplishment, where we feel safe from the unknown. And it is a fear of the unknown, of what we cannot control, that perhaps frightens and challenges us the most.

There is a true sense of comfort and control when we find a place that we perceive as less threatening—in other words, less likely to change. It must be recognized and embraced that change within a congregation is inevitable. People move into the community, children are born, preachers leave and arrive, elders are added and resign, people pass away, and all of that elicits change in one or more ways within the normalcy of the congregation. Shawchuck and Heuser insist, "The only congregations that will thrive in the coming decades will be those whose leaders have learned to respond to change, not resist or ignore it."[1]

Change is a reaction to circumstances. It comes in both positive and negative climates and in large and small congregations. It is not necessarily a negative thing, but is often seen to be negative because it forces action when action may not be desired. Change is not the friend of the complacent or apathetic, nor of those who like things the way they are. Of course, none of these feelings are beneficial to congregational growth and effective ministry. A congregation filled with the complacent, apathetic, and "set in their ways" is a congregation that will find it difficult to grow spiritually and numerically or will have a low level of participation and volunteerism. So, change can be positive, a symbol of progress, and must be accepted and embraced. Congregational leaders should be aware of the inevitability of change and seek to manage it in an effective way.

Change arises in two ways. First, change comes as a result of unavoidable situations. Negative things happen to good people and good congregations. Members are lost through conflict,[2] employment, family crises, and any number of other circumstances. Decisions are made that may not work out as planned, so negative results occur. In other words, despite the best efforts and plans, negative things will occur, and when the leadership embraces that simple fact, the better their efforts to lead.

Change that comes from unavoidable circumstances is often difficult to accept, perhaps more so than from other causes, for it

---

[1] Shawchuck and Heuser, *Leading the Congregation*, 167.

[2] I will discuss conflict and its resolution in greater detail in chapter eight.

is seen to reflect imperfections and poor performance either in the church's leadership, ministry staff, the congregation as a whole, or in social issues that often hamper a congregation's progress. For example, the congregation on First Street is forced to make changes to its ministry staff due to human frailty and sin, or the Main Street church must abandon its plans for foreign missions because of a loss of financial resources due to a recession in the local economy. Maybe change is necessitated by decreasing attendance due to the departure of several families after an internal conflict. Whatever the cause, change that comes from unforeseen, difficult, and unavoidable circumstances can be a bitter pill to swallow because of the feeling of a loss of control and power.

Second, change occurs due to specific efforts on the part of congregational leadership. These are efforts associated with a "fresh perspective" or "a new way of thinking." Sometimes intentional change comes as a reaction to conflict, but usually it comes from what is perceived as poor performance, unacceptable numbers, or ineffective programs, arising from statements such as, "We've got to make some changes around here." Similar in scope to the previous reason for change, this is change due to circumstances beyond the control of the congregation as a whole, but it is intentional where the leadership seeks to find a better way, a new path that will move them out of their present condition and toward an improvement of their situation.

In addition, intentional change can be the result of little or no conflict, but merely the desire and the need to improve, the result of forward-thinking leaders. While there may be a desire to move beyond what is seen to be mundane, archaic, or ineffective, there are no real problems but only a desire to move in another, better direction. For example, such change may be as simple as switching the type of songbook used in worship, altering the order of worship, or changing the times of worship. On the other hand, such changes may be something more complex, such as redoing the congregation's educational program, altering the methods of community evangelism, moving the entire congregation into a new building, on a new location, or a change in the location and scope of foreign missions.

The simple point of change is that regardless of the circumstances—unavoidable, unfortunate circumstances or the desire to move in a different, more effective direction—change carries within it a component of intentionality. The leadership, and the congregation who support the decision-making process, intends to make changes and seeks the means to do so. Organizations, and the organization that is the congregation, face a fear of change, yet without the effect of change, congregations become stagnant and cease to continue along the path of renewal. On the other hand, change for its own sake leads to instability, causing leaders, participants, and resources to be stretched thin.[3]

In this chapter I want to focus on change that is intentionally initiated, whether from the unforeseen, unfortunate circumstances within the human experience or through the need to improve and develop. In other words, I want to focus on change that is the conscious, orchestrated effort of servant leadership to move forward, develop forward, and motivate forward, change that intentionally makes people move, work, and improve. I choose to do this because that element of change emerges as a valuable tool of leaders and followers.

The implementation of change is an element of strategic thinking because it implies intentional, planned, and sometimes aggressive action. Hogan defined it rather simply: "To change

---

[3] George D. Parsons and Speed B. Leas, "Creative Tension in Congregational Life: Beyond Homeostasis," in *Conflict management in Congregations*, ed. David B. Lott (Bethesda, MD: The Alban Institute, 2001), 62–63.

something is to make it different from what it has been. It is to modify, alter, or vary."[4] Hogan's definition touches on one of the more common reasons change is frightening to some: making something different than it has been. Congregations often face this when they have existed for many decades and still enjoy the presence of some of their original members and/or succeeding generations from the original members. What occurs is a change in generational ideals and the disheartened cry, "That's not the way we always did that!" The issue may be as fundamental as the use of gospel meetings (something abandoned by many congregations today), methods of community evangelism (door-knocking and/or leafleting), or the hiring of a ministry staff (e.g. youth, education, or involvement). It may be something as simple as which songbook to use, plastic or glass communion cups, padded or unpadded pews, or a wooden or acrylic pulpit stand.

The issue of change, and the fear or embracing of it, can be a generational issue, for each generation has a different perspective from the others on how things ought to be done. Congregational leaders should be aware of the reality of generational differences and their impact on the implementation of change as a facet of strategic thinking. Ian Fair helps us understand the phenomenon, so I will borrow from him and then add a point or two of my own:

The **G.I. Generation** (64–92 in 1993) came of age during the Depression, so they carry a frugal, no-nonsense mentality. They tend to be institutionally inclined, so they support that which they are a part of: church, country, and civic organization. They also tend to work together, be civic-minded, and team players. They are pragmatic, conformists, male-dominated, and are likely to trust in the government and institutional authority. They usually do not support the Silent Generation and distrust the Boom-

---

[4] Norman Hogan, *Leadership in the Local Church* (Henderson, TN: Nakari Publications, 1988), 59.

ers. (In addition to Fair's information, I will add that, within their congregation, they are either movers and shakers, or they feel lost and out-of-touch).

The **Silent Generation** (48–63 in 1993) tends to be interested in the system and not the individual (the congregation over the preacher, elder, deacon, or whoever). They usually seek to defuse conflict, tend to be flexible, and are suspicious of grand and lofty ideals (new congregational programs). They prefer order, rigidity, and duty. They tend to prefer participation over authority (elders who change things are not appreciated) and process over results (attendance numbers are not important as long as the congregation is doing something).

The **Baby Boom Generation or Boomers** (29–47 in 1993) tend to be suspicious of institutionalism. They (we, for I am a Boomer) generated Woodstock, violent revolutionary action, and open protest. They were raised in one of the most affluent periods in our nation's history and tend to be smug, confident, and critical. They are concerned with principles. They distrust any older generation, perhaps more so with of the G.I. Generation. They seek to balance self-esteem and self-indulgence. They embrace religion, but reject institutional, corporate religion, leaning toward individualistic, internal religions. They tend to reject anything gender-oriented or authority-based. They were "hippies" or were raised within the influence of "hippies." They mistrust and tend to be a bit paranoid with "Big Brother," "Big Business," and "Big Government."

The **Baby Buster Generation** (1–28 in 1993) is the so-called "Generation X" or "GenX." They are the products of the Boomers. They tend to be brash and "in-your-face." They tend to be somewhat lazier than former generations, especially the Silent Generation, but hold on to big dreams. They tend to be pessimistic, dismissive, and noncommittal. They tend to be driven by appetites and not ideals, so they show little concern for doing good rather than feeling good. Commitment to education, careers, and "pulling your own weight" is much less in this generation. They tend to disbelieve in absolutes. Their entertainment world is dominated by dysfunctional families, dead-beat or clueless dads, social chaos, and extreme violence and sexuality. In the same way, cynicism, poverty, and violence are normal aspects of their society (1 out of every 5 of them live in these conditions). They tend to be oriented toward money.

Of course, Fair's information is a bit dated (1993), for an entire generation, sometimes called the **Computer Generation**, is left out. They represent those of the Baby Buster Generation who have since had children of their own. With that new generation come new ideals and outlooks, new methods and worldviews. They will be the future leaders, preachers, and teachers of congregations throughout the country and even throughout the world. How will they react to change and its implications? Will they retreat from it as did those of a few generations ago or embrace, even run toward it, as do their parents and others among the Baby Buster Generation?

When congregational servant leaders are aware of these differences and accept their place within every congregation, they will be able to lead through the tool of intentional change, in spite of the unforeseen and unfortunate. This is easier said than done, but it must be done nonetheless. Congregations of today are not the congregations of yesteryear in a variety of ways. People no longer attend the church in their immediate community, but will travel thirty, forty, fifty, or sixty minutes to attend the congregation that suits them best. Small towns have been absorbed by larger cities and metropolitans have been formed. The concepts and realities of neighborhood, friendliness, and family have changed. People sit behind closed, even locked, doors instead of on front porches. The emergence and development of social media has done little to make us more social, but has isolated us into chat rooms, pages of interest, and so on. We "talk" all the time and are willing to share almost everything, but we no longer do it face-to-face. We have come to treasure our privacy and isolation in the midst of so much "sharing."

Imagine how the emergence of the computer age and a computer-driven society has changed how congregations approach their work, such as evangelism. What has always been done to reach the lost may or may not work in a community glued to their computers, notebooks, and cell phone screens. At the same time, leafleting and door-knocking, as well as mass-mailing through the Postal Service, have been replaced in some circles by email. Bible studies are no longer conducted at any given moment through a personal face-to-face experience but through the face-to-face experience of Skype or something similar.

The internet has brought tremendous change within our society and that has significantly influenced our congregations, and when the leaders realize and embrace this, they will be able to shepherd the flock much more effectively. They must do this through the proper and effective use of change, either by embracing the changes that occur that are beyond our control or intentionally developing changes that are by design. By being aware of the generations and their perspectives on procedure and practice within our congregations, as well as their idiosyncrasies, strengths and weaknesses, congregational leaders can sculpt change for the benefit of all involved.

Jesus was all about change, and His ministry was permeated with it. He changed the way the multitudes thought about spiritual leaders when He spoke as one with authority and not like the scribes and Pharisees (Mt. 7.28–29). He changed the lives and perspectives of His apostles, taking the commonplace (fishermen), the controversial (a tax-collector), and a host of other professions and life choices. He took the fears, apprehensions, disillusions, and misunderstandings of the disciples and changed those emotions into faith, conviction, and ministry: Peter turns from frightened denial to impassioned preaching, Saul turns from a zealous persecutor to Paul the missionary, and Thomas turns from skepticism to proclamation.

Of course, Jesus, in bringing so much change, angered many who heard His teaching and witnessed His ministry. He was constantly questioned, threatened, and accused by the scribes, Pharisees, chief priests, and elders. His consistent effectiveness caused them to become very jealous of Jesus. Even though they were the spiritual leaders of the people who should have led the multitudes to the Messiah, their reactions stemmed from their selfishness, ignorance, and arrogance.

Among the churches of Christ, and perhaps within some of the denominations, a term has been coined that receives a two-sided response. The term is *change agent,* and over the past several years it has been viewed as either the harbinger of necessary progress or the path to unscriptural practice, depending upon the source. The negative side of *change agent* is obvious, for we are commanded to conduct ourselves in life and worship according to the standards laid down by the Lord (cf. Mt. 28.20), but there are those who desire change unauthorized in Scripture.

In this discussion of spiritual leadership, *change agent* refers to what is beneficial and scriptural for the practices and development of congregations. In the same way *change agent* is used negatively, it is also a term used for leaders who bring about beneficial changes in the congregations they serve. Good leaders will bring about beneficial change for their congregations without scriptural, doctrinal, and ethical compromise.

Leaders who would bring about beneficial change were needed in the church in Corinth, for their spiritual problems were numerous. Paul's encouragement to them was couched within those problems: "I am glad about the coming of Stephanus, Fortunatus, and Achaicus, for what was lacking on your part they supplied. For they refreshed my spirit and yours; therefore acknowledge such men" (1 Cor. 16.17–18). These men sought to bring beneficial change to a congregation permeated with spiritual disrepair. In essence, they became agents of change to lead that congregation in a proper direction.

Paul himself became an agent of beneficial change for the church. As he recounted his conversion before Agrippa, he stated that the Lord said to him, "But arise and stand on your feet; for I have appeared to you for this purpose, to make you a minister and a witness both of the things which you have seen and of the things which I will yet reveal to you. I will deliver you from the Jewish people, as well as from the Gentiles, to whom I now send you, to open their eyes and to turn them from darkness to light, and from the power of Satan to God, that they may receive forgiveness of sins and inheritance among those who are sanctified by faith in Me" (Acts 26.16–18). Paul was to bring wide-sweeping changes through his commission from the Lord.

Timothy was also an agent of change for the church in Ephesus. Paul instructed Timothy to "Preach the word! Be ready in reason and out of season. Convince, rebuke, exhort, with all longsuffering" (2 Tim. 4.2). Paul goes on to warn Timothy of those who would "not endure sound doctrine" and would "turn their ears away from the truth" (3–4). So, Paul instructs Timothy, "But you be watchful in all things, endure afflictions, do the work of an evangelist, fulfill your ministry" (5).

Earlier I emphasized how frightening and intimidating change can be to a congregation, but bringing about beneficial change is not only frightening for the congregation, but also for the leadership as well. That fear and intimidation are why many leaders and congregations do not embrace change. Again, it is a fear of the unknown and the unexpected, even though the unknown and unexpected could be positive, and many are skeptical of what they feel they cannot control and they feel they cannot control the unexpected. Even more are skeptical of anything that they feel will remove them from their comfort zone. To them, change equals a lack of what has become routine, knowable, predictable, and comfortable.

Change, when considered properly, is indicative of challenge, and knowing that can help remove its stigma. Kouzes and Posner offered three observations on change and challenge:[5]

1. People who become leaders do not always seek the challenges they face. Challenges also seek leaders.
2. Opportunities to challenge the status quo and introduce change open the doors to doing one's best. Challenge is the motivating environment for excellence.
3. Challenging opportunities often bring forth skills and abilities that people do not know they have. Given the opportunity and the support, ordinary managers can get extraordinary things done in organizations.

Even though Kouzes and Posner write with secular organizations in mind, consider how their observations fit the congregational scheme. The first observation—"People who become leaders do not always seek the challenges they face. Challenges also seek leaders"—describes, in part, many who are elders in congregations around the nation and the world. They were chosen perhaps

---

[5] Kouzes and Posner, *The Leadership Challenge*, 39.

because of their age, business experience, or likeability (or any combination thereof) and gave little or no thought to the awesome responsibility they had accepted. In essence, they do little more than fill a space in their shepherding duties. Peter encouraged elders to "shepherd the flock of God...serving as overseers... nor as being lords over those entrusted to you, but being examples to the flock" (1 Pet. 5.1–3). Peter perhaps responded to elders he knew or knew of who took their responsibilities less seriously than they should or who felt their shepherding was all about control and power and not service.

The second and third observations of Kouzes and Posner—challenge as a motivating environment for excellence, as well as challenge as a way to reveal skills and abilities previously unknown—relate to what often arises when change is implemented and managed properly. First, the congregation is challenged to increase their potential and do their best to improve and develop, but the fear of change threatens their comfort zone and their desire for what is routine. Yet, meeting the challenge forces them to be stretched beyond what is comfortable and routine. People who have refused to teach become teachers, people who have not become involved become involved, and people who have never taken charge begin to take charge.

Change can often be a necessary step in good leadership when it seeks to benefit the congregation as a whole. While some seek to change the methods and practices of the congregation in unscriptural and even unethical ways, good leaders will seek change only when change is necessary and reflective of their commission to be the spiritual leaders of the congregation as servants of the Lord. This becomes a tremendous challenge, not only for the leadership, but for the congregation as a whole. It is a challenge because it forces action and activity.

When seen from its various perspectives, change becomes a tool of vision and mission; after all, the casting of a vision and the statement of mission are intended to improve, develop, and motivate, all of which are elements of change. At the same time, intentional change—that which moves the congregation past the unforeseen and unfortunate or that which improves the congregation and its effectiveness—is something that must cast a vision and state its mission as well.

Kotter, writing from an entirely secular, business point-of-view—still relevant to our concerns of congregational leadership and change—developed an eight-stage process of change.[6] I will borrow a few processes from his list and offer a few thoughts, but allow you, the reader, to make appropriate applications as you apply them to your own situation. First, leaders of change will establish a sense of urgency.[7] As I stated earlier, change is frightening and daunting to many, and even though the congregation accepts the need for change, they may not be eager to begin the process quickly, so complacency becomes a problem. Congregations tend to push aside what needs to be done and tabling important decisions and processes that would force such change to begin. Leaders of change must build confidence and acceptance that lead to the urgency to get down to business.

---

[6] Kotter, *Leading Change*, 1996. I will use only five of the eight in Kotter's list. Chapter seven, "Empowering Employees for Broad-based Action," addresses, for our purposes, the concern of empowerment and I discussed that earlier. Chapter nine, "Consolidating Gains and Producing More Change," address that issues and concerns that have a minor connection to the focus of this book and is better observed through a secular, business lens. Chapter ten, "Anchoring New Approaches in the Culture" offers something relatively new in leadership studies, "Cultural Intelligence," which I find absolutely fascinating actually. While congregations have a "culture," to discuss it in the context of this book would move us into much a larger study and beyond the scope of what I am doing in this book about servant leadership. I will mention it again briefly in chapter seven in regard to the congregation as an organized system.

[7] Ibid., chapter three, 35–49.

Second, leaders of change must create "the guiding coalition."[8] This is the stage of the change process in which leaders establish a body of force to guide and direct the church in the proper direction.

Kotter warned against assuming that "the kind of leadership that is so critical to any change can come only from a single larger-than-life person."[9] In the secular world, such larger-than-life persons are seen in the examples and influences of men such as Rockefeller, Vanderbilt, Ford, and others in the industrial age. . . Kotter cites Lee Iacocca and Chrysler Corporation and Sam Walton of Walmart as examples from a more modern era.[10] These examples and hundreds more form a framework of larger-than-life leaders who were indicative of a Big Man leadership style and phenomenon.

Congregations certainly make such assumptions, perhaps due to a larger-than-life elder who is expected to push them through, again. Delegation and empowerment, or a lack thereof, become foundational issues of the problem, for too little is done in some locations because of the types of leadership that micromanage, are distrustful of others, or a combination of both (as well as other negative leadership types). If congregations will develop and thrive, it will—it must— be done through the machinations of a body of leaders, movers, and shakers: a guiding coalition, "a powerful force [that is] required to sustain the process."[11]

Third, leaders of change will develop a vision and strategy of change.[12] Just as a vision must be cast and a strategy of implementation must be established in all aspects of leadership, so it must be done in regard to intentional, necessary change. Kotter

---

[8] Ibid., chapter four, 51–66.

[9] Ibid., 51.

[10] Ibid.

[11] Ibid.

[12] Ibid., chapter five, 67–83.

offered three purposes of casting a good vision: (1) clarification of the general direction for change; (2) motivation of the people to take action; (3) efficient coordination of the actions of different people. As I wrote in chapter four, "Vision Casting and Mission," and chapter five, "Strategy and Implementation," three key elements of vision casting are (1) envisioning and portraying a *picture* of what is proposed, (2) projecting the vision into the future, and (3) empowering and equipping the people who will implement the vision. When these things are done, the necessary steps are taken to ensure a measure of efficiency and success.

Fourth, leaders of change will effectively communicate the vision of change.[13] Kotter commented, "A great vision can serve a useful purpose even if it is understood by just a few key people. But the real power of a vision is unleashed only when most of those involved in an enterprise or activity have a common understanding of its goals and direction."[14] As with the overall vision that is cast for the future of the congregation, the success for a vision of change increases as the numbers of people who are able to implement it increase as well.

I recall a Bible camp in a southern state years ago that had developed a "work week" of encampment that offered the campers the opportunity to work to improve the physical condition of the camp. A man was given the task of supervising a portion of the repairs and improvements needed for the upcoming encampment season and was given a team of dozen or so teens to assist him. As they gathered on the first morning to begin their work, he informed them that what they were about to do was perhaps the most dangerous work needing to be done (primarily the work involved climbing on ladders, and hanging speakers and their wires). Needless to say, the excitement and commitment of

---

[13] Ibid, chapter six, 85–100.

[14] Ibid., 85.

that group of teens diminished tremendously. Communication, of course, was the problem, for his summary of their part of the vision of improving the camp was more than they wished to do. A few of us pulled him aside and suggested he delegate the climbing of ladders and the hanging of speakers and their wires to those who could and would do so; there would be plenty of work for the others that did not require such labor. Then, we suggested that he tell them why they would carry out the task—for example, communication throughout the camp property and music that could be played during free time—and how their week(s) of encampment would improve once they completed the job. The result was a team of teens who worked well together and accomplished the task they were assigned.

Fifth, leaders of change will empower the workers for what they are to do.[15] Of course, I wrote of empowerment in the general vision that is cast for the congregation in chapter seven. As in the overall vision of the congregation, those who carry out the vision of intentional, beneficial change must be given what they need to complete their part in the task.

Sixth, Kotter suggested that leaders of change will generate short-term wins.[16] I really like this point because it applies to both the overall vision of the congregation, as well as a vision for intentional, efficient change. In addition, it is something too often not included in the casting and implementation of vision. As I noted in chapter five, I have waited until now to discuss this essential element of vision casting.

The benefit of offering short-term wins to the congregation is to allow all involved to see the progress being made and to feel a sense of accomplishment through the arduous task of implementing the vision. During the writing of this book, my wife and

---

[15] Ibid, chapter seven , 101–115.

[16] Ibid, chapter eight, 117–130.

I, along with our oldest daughter and our two granddaughters aged five years and fifteen months, moved from southern Indiana to southern California, a journey of well over 1900 miles. Faced with such a daunting task, we decided to break the distance up by making reservations at various campgrounds between points A and B which offered a comfortable setting as well as events to look forward to (e.g. visit with friends and family and site seeing). Along the way, our oldest granddaughter was a real trooper, in spite of the long days of driving and pulling an RV. We explained to her our destination at the end of each day, and what we would do and see once we arrived. In addition, we also reminded her of our final destination—our goal in completing the journey—and what she could expect once we settled in a new state. Our arduous, long journey was broken into manageable *short-term wins* as we gradually moved closer to the final goal.

The idea that something will change petrifies some within any congregation because of it being viewed as a harbinger of inadequate, inefficient, and weak leadership and followership, and it may be within a given circumstance. Change, however, should be expected, even embraced, if it is seen as a means by which improvements will be made and a vision of a brighter future is proclaimed.

Shawchuck and Heuser wrote, "[The] congregation that does not change to meet the changes in its environment....will soon find itself cut off, irrelevant, lost."[17] Change, when it is intentional and formative, is an envisioned plan to move into the future. Unexpected and detrimental change is inevitable, but the need to bring out change to continue to work effectively is also inevitable. Shawchuck and Heuser concluded their chapter on congregational renewal by insisting that, "The leader sets the tone for and helps to create the conditions in which the congre-

---

[17] Shawchuck and Heuser, *Leading the Congregation*, 211.

gation is equipped and encouraged to study its future with anticipation, to encourage and support innovative ministries, and to aspire to excellence in all the large and small ministries of the church. This is what it means to manage change, rather than to be managed by it."[18]

---

[18] Ibid., 181.

SEVEN | *Issues of Leadership*

In this chapter, I will change the lens of the discussion from the issues of vision, mission, strategy, and change. Now, I will consider some of the problems that arise when leadership is done and congregations function as the organizations they are. By changing the lens of our study, I do not mean to imply we are leaving any considerations of vision and mission, strategy and implementation, or the place and function of change, behind. Instead, I am increasing the magnification to look more closely into the organization called the congregation.

The substance of this chapter is considered in four parts: (1) Spiritual Growth and Formation, (2) Congregational Numerical Plateauing, (3) Conflict and Resolution, and (4) Ineffective Elders'/Business Meetings. Before I discuss those four concerns of leadership, I will begin with some brief observations regarding the congregation as a system and an organization.[1]

The Systemic Organization that is a Congregation

It may surprise, shock, and even anger some to think of a congregation as something organizational or a system, but it is. Such

---

[1] The purpose is to briefly introduce the concept of system and systems theory, and make a few observations.

an emotional response may arise from failing to understand the idea of a system and how systems theory can be used to comprehend the work place and function of a congregation. A simple way to grasp the idea of the system of an organization is the human body: the nervous system, the circulatory system, the digestive system. Each of us understands the dynamics of the human body as a system and recognizes how our bodies as a system work and are to be best maintained.

In his first epistle to a deeply troubled and spiritually bereft congregation, the apostle Paul spoke of the church as a body and emphasized it as an organized system:

> For just as the body is one and has many members, and all the members of the body, though many, are one body, so it is with Christ. For in one Spirit we were all baptized into one body—Jews or Greeks, slaves or free—and all were made to drink of one Spirit. For the body does not consist of one member but of many. If the foot should say, "Because I am not a hand, I do not belong to the body," that would not make it any less a part of the body. And if the ear should say, "Because I am not an eye, I do not belong to the body," that would not make it any less a part of the body. If the whole body were an eye, where would be the sense of hearing? If the whole body were an ear, where would be the sense of smell? But as it is, God arranged the members in the body, each one of them, as he chose. If all were a single member, where would the body be? As it is, there are many parts, yet one body. The eye cannot say to the hand, "I have no need of you," nor again the head to the feet, "I have no need of you." On the contrary, the parts of the body that seem to be weaker are indispensable, and on those parts of the body that we think less honorable we bestow the greater honor, and our unpresentable parts are treated with greater modesty, which our more presentable parts do not require. But God has so composed the body, giving greater honor to the part that lacked it, that there may be no division in the body, but

that the members may have the same care for one another. If one member suffers, all suffer together; if one member is honored, all rejoice together. Now you are the body of Christ and individually members of it. And God has appointed in the church first apostles, second prophets, third teachers, then miracles, then gifts of healing, helping, administrating, and various kinds of tongues. Are all apostles? Are all prophets? Are all teachers? Do all work miracles? Do all possess gifts of healing? Do all speak with tongues? Do all interpret? But earnestly desire the higher gifts. And I will show you a still more excellent way (1 Cor. 12.12–31).

Paul's analysis of the church as a systemic, organized body is informative. He points out the specific tasks of individual body parts and how one cannot do the work of another, but each has its designed place and function. Key to Paul's analysis, for me, is the body of Christ as a collective, a group of individuals who work, move, interact, and connect with one another, supporting and sustaining one another, for if one is affected, so then is the whole.

To grasp the congregation as an organized system, an understanding of systems theory is helpful. Fremont Kast and James Rozenzweig wrote, "General systems theory emphasizes that systems are organized—they are composed of interdependent components in some relationship."[2] As in Paul's analogy of a congregation in 1 Corinthians 12, a system is an interconnected series (system) of parts that form the dynamic of a larger organization (the sum of the parts that form the whole). The leadership tool of systems theory makes sense of those parts and the whole.

Consider, then, Peter Steinke's definition: "System Theory is a way of conceptualizing reality. It organizes our thinking from a specific vantage point. System thinking considers the

---

[2] Fremont E. Kast and James E. Rozenzweig, "General Systems Theories: Applications for Organizations and Management," *Academy of management Journal*, vol. 15, no. 4 (December 1972), 74.

interrelatedness of the parts. Instead of seeing isolated, unrelated parts, we look at the whole....System thinking deepens our understanding of life. We see it as a rich complexity of interdependent parts. Basically, a system is a set of forces and events that interact, such as a weather system or the solar system. To think systemically is to look at the ongoing, vital interaction of the connected parts."[3]

Steinke also emphasized that the concept of a system is concerned with reality rather than "a tidy theory."[4] It is the way things *really are* rather than how we want them to be or believe they are. In a way, this entire chapter addresses issues that must see the reality of things rather than what they are in theory. In a way, systems theory allows leaders to see what is happening *as a whole*. Systems theory helps leaders to see mutual influences, causation, and connectivity. As Steinke put it, "System theory teaches us to think of loops instead of lines,"[5] and I find that very informative. He differentiated between *straight-line thinking* (one direction, A to B) and *system thinking* (loops, A and B). He diagramed it this way:

Fig. 6- A reproduction of Steinke's Straight Line and System thinking

---

[3] Peter L. Steinke, *How Your Church Family Works: Understanding Congregations as Emotional Systems* (Bethesda, MD: The Alban Institute, 1993), 3, 4.

[4] Ibid., 3.

[5] Steinke, *How Your Church Family Works*, 4.

When put into practice, what does system thinking, thinking systemically, look like? Basically, it observes action and reaction: what happened and why it happened. "Action provides information. People respond or react to it."[6] Instead of focusing on "what" (What was the cause; what was the effect?), the focus would be on action-response-action-response. Steinke alluded to the example of kicking a stone versus kicking a dog, cited by therapist Lynn Hoffman. When the stone is kicked, it moves in the direction of the kick based on its weight and the force of the kick. "The stone doesn't shout, 'Why did you kick me?'" When one kicks a dog, however, "there is a counter-move. The dog may cringe and look hurt, run away, bark menacingly, or lurch forward to attack. There is now information and relatedness. The kicker may scowl, retreat, shout, or rethink his kicking behavior."[7]

Another aspect of thinking systemically is "how interactions are mutually influenced and how they become patterned or repeated." Steinke uses the political system as an example: "Candidates make sweeping promises that they could never possibly fulfill. The electorate wants more from their elected elders than they could actually give. The two parts are interrelated. The politician's outlandish pledge and the electorate's fanciful desires form a pattern of behavior."[8]

Congregational leaders will do well to observe their congregations systemically rather than linearly. As shepherds of the flock, they will benefit from seeing more than just mere cause and effect (e.g. who started the rumor and what problems arose), but the interrelationships, influences, and mutuality of those involved, as well as how such interrelationships and interactions are repeated.

---

[6] Ibid., 5.

[7] Ibid.

[8] Steinke, *How Your Church Family Works*, 6.

In connection to the congregation as a system, one of the relatively recent topics of research and discussion to emerge within leadership studies is *cultural intelligence*, which I noted briefly in chapter six. Drury reminds us that "not every collection of people develops a culture. It is only formed when there has been enough shared history for the people to become a group rather than a crowd."[9] Congregations can certainly have a culture, and leaders must embrace it and learn how to understand and use it.

Schein, a leading researcher in organizational culture, defined it as "a pattern of shared basic assumptions that the group learned as it solved its problems of external adaptation and internal integration, that has worked well enough to be considered valid and therefore, to be taught to new members as the correct way to perceive, think, and feel in relation to these problems."[10] Put simply, and for the purposes of this chapter, an organization's culture is identified through the way it functions, how it shares and utilizes information, key players within its dynamics, the way conflicts and problems are handled, and so on.

Leaders will do well to recognize a congregation's cultural dynamics. For example, who is the better source of internal information like congregational satisfaction, personality conflict, and so on: the secretary, the youth minister, one of the song leaders, or the couple who sits on the left aisle, seven rows from the front? Who would be best suited to build momentum for a new program of church growth: one of the elders, the pulpit minister, one of the deacons, or the man who was the preacher for more than twenty years, thirty years ago? Which one of the elders is best capable to push *that* program idea through, which one of the deacons can best implement *that* physical plant program, and which member(s) have the best community contacts for *that* idea? Who

---

[9] Drury, *Handbook*, 52.

[10] Edgar Schein, *Organizational culture*, 12.

are congregation's assets and liabilities, who are the most dependable and least so; who make the best volunteers, who have the congregation's best interests at heart, and who express the more positive attitudes? Who are the fringe and who make up the core? Who will run away at the first sign of tension and failure, and who will stick with the spiritual family through thick and thin?

Congregational servant leaders will be more efficient and capable when they are aware of these cultural phenomena within the flock they shepherd, for knowing these things, and more, can potentially remove doubts, uncertainties, and the undetermined. The culture of a congregation is a part of its pulse, its dynamic ebb and flow, and its patterns of behavior, both positive and negative.

Spiritual Growth and Formation

It seems that everyone has a plan for nurturing the spiritual growth and formation of a congregation. Seminars, workshops, conferences, classes, newsletters, books, and articles all lay claim to a formula for success. Methodological tools range from door-to-door studies and advertising, using community mailing lists, *seeker's* classes, special events such as gospel meetings and teaching seminars, friendship evangelism/contagious Christianity, and the list goes on and on.

The spiritual and numerical growth of a congregation should be of significance to its leadership. In fact, all that has been discussed in this book thus far, and what will be discussed in the remainder of this chapter affects, in one way or the other, positively or negatively, the growth of a congregation. In Acts 2.42–47, Luke indicated that after the three thousand were added on the day of Pentecost, the disciples "devoted themselves to the apostles' teaching and the fellowship, to the breaking of bread and the prayers" (42) and that "all who believed were together and had all things in common" (43) as they praised God, "having favor with all the people. And the Lord added to their number day by day those who were being saved" (47). Of course, we are familiar with Paul's summary of evangelism: "I planted, Apollos watered, but God gave the growth" (1 Cor. 3.6).

These passages and so many more affirm the desire for and the necessity of congregational growth both spiritually and numerically. The problem with many, if not most, of these plans and formulas is little or no differentiation between spiritual and numerical growth; too many equate success and efficiency with larger numbers. Many seem drawn to the stories of congregations that have grown from one hundred to three hundred and more in only a few years or congregations that boast attendance numbers over one thousand. I believe it unwise to base the desire for church growth on the success stories of other congregations, for their success may be due to a number of circumstances:

1. Sometimes a congregation will grow numerically because of offering a given program and implementing a given plan at just the right time. Sales and marketing professionals will agree that timing is often the key to success and often it is no different within congregations. So then, while a program works well for the Main Street congregation, it may not be the right time for the First Street congregation to implement due to any number of circumstances.

2. Sometimes a congregation that has grown numerically owes much of their increase to what is called *swelling* or a sudden and substantial increase in numbers, especially for a Sunday morning worship service. This is true in areas where there are several congregations in close proximity. When problems arise, members of a given congregation seek the higher ground by transferring to another con-

gregation. In this way, that congregation may grow by a hundred or two hundred percent, or more. Other congregations see this increase and, as is so common, equate the increase in attendance to efficient and productive evangelism when it occurred primarily due to circumstances.

3. Sometimes a congregation may grow numerically because of something new, gimmicky, or popular. These things reside predominately in congregations that favor the theatrical or spectacular, or in congregations that feature the preaching of a market-oriented preacher. These congregations enjoy much of their growth through an audience wishing to see something they perceive as awe-inspiring, and so participate in the spectacle. In reality, if numerical growth occurred primarily due to the introduction of something new and/or theatrical, then they may require something even newer and more theatrical to maintain the audience they have.

Each of these circumstances allows plenty of room for bragging-rights but little room for legitimate, healthy spiritual growth, and will not suffice for servant leaders who have the best interests of the congregation at heart. In my opinion, healthy spiritual growth is the result of a determined strategy for implementing the congregation's vision and mission, and not the result of circumstances. I will admit that an increase in numbers can provide a foundation for healthy growth—an increase in resources for example—but that foundation is extremely unstable if it is left to stand on its own.

I have often wondered how many other churches wanted to be more like the congregation at Ephesus. They had good works and labors for the sake of the Lord's name, commendable patience, and their reputation of intolerance for evil people, their testing of false apostles, their perseverance, and their lack of weariness (Rev. 2.2-3). They had a problem, however, for they had lost their first love—they put up a good facade, but were only going through the motions (4). Using contemporary examples, they were the congregation that had a large (maybe the largest) modern building, a large (maybe the largest) Sunday morning attendance, a fleet of vans and buses emblazoned with the name of the congregation on their sides, visitor-friendly programs of outreach, creative methods of preaching and teaching, and a host of other programs, amenities, and opportunities. Perhaps they set the bar that measures success higher merely because of how they appeared to be. How many modern churches seek to pattern themselves after others they feel are more successful and growing numerically based merely on outward appearances?

Notice that I have emphasized the issue of *numerical* growth, often the source of some envy and the subject of emulation. It is a mistake to focus only on an increase in numbers because a congregation is to grow spiritually *and* numerically. I am of the opinion that when the former, spiritual growth, is engaged properly, it will contribute to the success of the latter, numerical growth. The measure of success, however, is too often the numbers and not hearts surrendered to Jesus Christ.

I believe we have gotten the cart before the horse when we emphasize the size of the congregation's Sunday morning attendance rather than the congregation's spiritual health. It has been assumed by many that if a congregation is of a certain number,[11] they must be successful. When congregational leaders buy into such thinking, they are automatically sapped of some of their

---

[11] The number is somewhat arbitrary—200, 300, 500, or 1000. Often the number associated with success and efficiency is relative to the area. If most of the congregations average in the 90s or up to 150, a congregation of 300 might be the epitome of success. If most of the congregations average 200–300, then the model of success may need to be 500, 600, or more.

strength and resources for spiritual success because they are buying into only half of the bigger picture and not what the Bible emphasizes is most important.

One byproduct of poor (or a lack of) spiritual formation is the emergence of congregational stagnation. In general, "stagnant" is defined as "showing no activity, dull, sluggish."[12] I use the word *stagnation* because that is what a congregation in spiritual trouble does: it just sits there still and quiet with no forward movement or activity. Congregational stagnation is manifested in a variety of ways, including (1) decreased participation and volunteerism, (2) the reality of little more than going through the motions in regard to worship and fellowship, and (3) a sense of apathy toward unexpected twists and turns in congregational life.

Stagnation is difficult to recognize and even more difficult to correct without a clear understanding of and a motivation toward spiritual formation and the development of faith. Congregations may not recognize they are stagnant because what they have become may appear normal. Recall the "frog in a kettle" analogy. If a frog is placed in a kettle of boiling water, it will immediately try to escape, but if it is placed in a kettle of cool water and the water begins to gradually turn to boiling, it will not realize the danger until it is too late. Congregations must seek out spiritual growth and formation, or they will face the danger of becoming stagnant and gradually cease to function without any spiritual purpose, or even eventually die.

Spiritual formation and growth are both individual and congregational efforts.

Remember that Romans 12.1–2 is written not only to individuals, but to the assembly in Rome, so the principles of a holy and acceptable living sacrifice and the transformation of a renewed

---

[12] *Oxford Illustrated American Dictionary*, 806

mind must be applied congregationally. Leaders must focus the congregation in this direction—toward a greater spirituality.

The quest for greater spirituality is sometimes one of twists and turns, fraught with setbacks and gradual improvements alike. To deny this is to ignore the reality of the human experience, the positive and negative of human development, which includes the development of spirituality. In addition, the experience of spiritual formation is not just done individually, but is shared congregationally. In other words, what affects me will affect others, for I am a member of the congregation.

In a doctoral class on faith development, Dr. Everett Huffard commented, "We need to develop a language of spiritual defeat and the level of spiritual pain and tolerance in ministry."[13] His point is well-taken, for often spiritual formation and faith development are seen to be personal and not collective endeavors, yet the congregation as a whole faces the trials and enjoys the triumphs together. A way to communicate the ups and downs of ministry and spiritual living must be developed and utilized so the congregation will grow together through such spiritual experiences.[14]

This "language of spiritual defeat and the level of spiritual pain and tolerance" are communicated clearly in scripture. I believe one of the best examples is found in the seven churches of Asia Minor, according to Revelation 2–3. Notice in the list of seven churches there are two that receive nothing but commendation, Smyrna and Philadelphia, two receive nothing but condemnation, Sardis and Laodicea, and the other three receive both commendation and condemnation (Ephesus, Pergamos, and Thyatira). The

---

[13] Everett Huffard, "Faith Development and the Ministry of the Church: Class Notes," *Harding University Graduate School of Religion* (Memphis, TN), 2003.

[14] This concern will be addressed again later in the discussion of conflict.

two who are commended have one thing in common: faithful service in spite of obstacles (Rev. 2.9–10; 3.8). Instead of losing their focus (Ephesus), turning toward compromised doctrines (Pergamos and Thyatira), and being complacent (Sardis and Laodicea), Smyrna and Philadelphia remained strong, took advantage of opportunities, and committed a work worthy of the praise of Jesus Christ. They came to speak the language of spiritual defeat and pain and it resonated through their souls as a proclamation of their faith as a congregation.

The activities of the congregation become activities of collective spiritual formation and the development of faith, and the elders, with the deacons and preacher or ministry staff, must take the lead. Through worship and fellowship, a sense of a spiritual family arises to define who a congregation is and what it wants to do. There is an ever-present sense of renewal sweeping through the congregation as each individual faces the trials and triumphs of Christian living, and that becomes a part of the overall experiences of the congregation as a whole. When God is praised in worship, He is praised as many voices become one. When prayer is lifted, it is offered through the thoughts of one man who speaks for and with the assembly. As the word is proclaimed, each individual makes a connection to the message and then that is transferred, as one collective effort, into the needs, wants, and expectations of the congregation.

All of that is much easier said than done, right? You bet it is, and that becomes a challenge for the leadership as they direct the congregation in spiritual formation and the development of faith. Congregations rarely attain anything close to a collective sense of spiritual formation and development of faith—people are too busy and too preoccupied with their own lives. What emerges as a congregation is in reality a collection of small groups of varying sizes and inclinations. Elders and ministers form visitation groups, cell groups, small group ministries, special classes, fellowship groups arranged by age, and so on. Churches with adequate budgets hire involvement, education, and youth ministers to try and reach the congregation in creative ways. "Bring Your Neighbor Sunday," a gospel meeting, a spiritual seminar, entertainment and fun night, and many other special events are organized with the intention of waking people up and inciting greater participation.

All of those things are all well and good, and certainly have a legitimate place in the overall work of ministry, but none of it will work unless they are organized upon the foundation of a congregation that is being spiritually formed and developed in their faith. Too often, leaders try to repair a spiritually anemic congregation with new programs and activities, when the problem is in their spirituality and faith. Jesus warned against trying to patch an old garment with a piece of new cloth, which only makes the tear bigger, or putting new wine in old wineskins, causing the wineskin to break and lose all the wine (Mt. 9.16–17). In a similar way, a congregation will not and cannot properly carry out its growth and developmental programs with old, worn-out, and leaky spirituality.

Spiritual formation and the development of faith in congregations will be done when the servant leaders decide to grow the congregation spiritually from the inside out. That was part of the problem within the church in Corinth, for they sought to exist as a congregation filled with spiritual gifts and enrichment, and the desire for the confirmation and knowledge of Christ, but they failed to do so because they remained spiritual infants and carnal in their thinking (1 Cor. 1.4–8; 3.1–3). Once again, it is easier said than done, and that is why spiritual formation and the development of faith within the congregation as a whole is one of the most grueling and daunting tasks of congregational leadership. I have already pointed out Paul's struggle with the immaturity and carnality of Corinth, but consider also his struggle with the bewitchment of the Galatians (Gal. 1.6; 3.1), the disunity and dishonesty in Ephesus (Eph. 4.1–6, 25–32), and the carnality of the Colossian church (Col. 3.1–11).

How can the leadership of a congregation stimulate the spiritual formation and development of faith in the congregation as a whole? It is hard enough to do this individually, so doing so congregation-wide is even more difficult. I believe there is power in the fact that congregational leaders are biblically referred to as *shepherds*; the biblical shepherd is the model of what servant leadership is intended to be. Paul instructed the Ephesian elders, "Pay careful attention to yourselves and to all the flock, in which the Holy Spirit has made you overseers, to care for the church of God, which He obtained with His own blood" (Acts 20.28).

Servant leaders reflect the biblical model of shepherding and built into the concept of shepherding are the ideas of leading/guiding, equipping, and protecting, all of which are borne out clearly in Psalm 23. I examined Psalm 23 in chapter three, "Followership," but let us revisit this magnificent psalm and discuss its contributions to understanding the shepherd as leader/guide and protector. Once again, the psalm reads as follows:

> The LORD is my shepherd; I shall not want.
>   He makes me lie down in green pastures.
> He leads me beside still waters.
>   He restores my soul.
> He leads me in paths of righteousness
>   for his name's sake.
>
> Even though I walk through the valley of the shadow of death,
>   I will fear no evil,

> for you are with me;
> > your rod and your staff,
> > they comfort me.
>
> You prepare a table before m
> > in the presence of my enemies;
> you anoint my head with oil;
> > my cup overflows.
> Surely goodness and mercy shall follow me
> > all the days of my life,
> and I shall dwell in the house of the LORD
> > forever.

As a leader and guide, the shepherd sustains and maintains the flock, so that they "shall not want" (1). He leads/guides them to the pastures of green grass and the still, safe waters (1, 2). As a protector, the shepherd is there with the flock in times of danger and fear (4). The shepherd also equips the flock with restoration and righteousness (3), honor (5), and assurance (6). As does the shepherd of the psalms, so should the shepherds of the congregations do as well.

Of course, congregational leaders will do best to follow the example of servant leadership given so distinctly through the ministry, practice, and life of Jesus Christ. Throughout His ministry, He demonstrated several key elements of effective leadership:

1. Jesus mentored His disciples through setting a proper example. He demonstrated a life of prayer, how to reach the hearts of the spiritual hungry, and the importance of faith, hope, and promise. Peter, in his instructions to elders, told them to "shepherd the flock of God...not as being lords over those entrusted to you, but being examples to the flock" (1 Pet. 5.2–3).

2. Jesus constantly taught His disciples, as many times as it took for them to listen. Jesus was the very epitome of

patience and gentleness. As they traveled about, He constantly pointed out things around that would be essential to their own ministries. He did so privately and in public, wherever a lesson was to be learned. Paul made it clear that an elder must be able to teach and not a novice (1 Tim. 3.2, 6). Do we assume that he refers to classroom teaching or can we expand the point to insist that in teaching, Paul refers to their mentoring and instruction through example and guidance?

3. Jesus also gave His disciples room to grow. Do we assume that when Jesus warned Judas of his betrayal, Peter of his denial, and the disciples of their abandonment, that they had no choice in the matter? Jesus warned them of their potential—I insist it was potential—misdeeds, but allowed them to make their choices and fall if they would fall and stand if they would stand. How difficult it must have been to hang on the cross and realize that His disciples still did not comprehend what He was doing. Congregational leaders will do well to mentor and teach the congregation and then allow the congregation to stumble and fall and rise and walk in the journey toward spiritual formation and the development of faith.

4. Finally, Jesus prayed for His disciples. Of course, John 17 is a fine example. He prayed for their spiritual health, for their spiritual development, for their ability to do the task given them, and their faith in Him and in themselves. Congregational leaders must be men of prayer, not only for themselves and for one another, but for the congregation as a body of individuals and as an assembly, a community of faith. The congregation needs to know the leaders pray for them and why.

One of the most difficult tasks of congregational leadership is to help in the spiritual formation and development of faith in the congregation. It must be done, however, if the congregation will move steadily toward its potential.

Congregational Numerical Plateauing And Loss

By insisting earlier that the primary focus of congregational growth is spiritual and not numerical, I do not mean to exclude the issue of numerical growth. While it should never be a focus of congregational health (small congregations can be spiritually thriving and large congregations can be spiritually vacuous), fluctuating or decreasing numerical attendance can be a symptom of problems, especially if attendance numbers begin to decline for no apparent reason. I emphasize the word *apparent* because for every result there is a reason, but sometimes the reason may not be so apparent.

Numerical plateauing or loss can be a symptom of a larger, more crucial issue, or it can be the result of naturally occurring circumstances within the life of a congregation. It is essential that congregational leaders know the difference. A congregation's attendance numbers might plateau or decrease, for instance, due to the relocation of families due to employment, the military, retirement, or family circumstances. The first congregation I served was in a Florida retirement community, which meant any number of individuals moving into the area and, so then, the potential for numerical growth. At the same time, however, the job market in the area suffered a severe decrease and many of the younger families were forced to move to find employment.

There are less than benign reasons a congregation's attendance numbers might plateau or decrease:

1. Dissatisfaction with the present ministry of the congregation. Perhaps some members feel the ministry efforts are sluggish or misdirected.
2. Discontent with the leadership of the congregation. I have already mentioned several negative, ineffective methods of leadership and such methodologies can drive people away.
3. Disagreement with worship styles or a sense of apathy toward the way worship is done.
4. Discontent with the preaching done in worship. Perhaps some feel the preaching is bland and mundane, they feel it lacks creativity, or their discontent lies somewhere in-between.
5. Discontent with the teaching/education programs within the congregation. Perhaps some feel little effort is made to produce quality biblical education, they feel the classes offered are too advanced for the congregation, or their discontent lies somewhere in between.

There are a variety of reasons a congregation will face a decline or a plateau in its attendance numbers and those listed above represent only a few.

The list above, however, addresses the issue of numerical decline more than perhaps numerical plateauing. It is obvious that numerical decline is a more serious problem than plateauing, but that is not to say that plateauing is not to be something of concern for the congregation and its leadership. While numerical decline is a sign of some sort of congregational malfunction, numerical plateauing might be a sign of congregational apathy or stagnation. The churches in Sardis and Laodicea were prime candidates for numerical plateauing, for Sardis was dead spiritually (Rev. 3.1) and Laodicea was lukewarm, felt they needed nothing, and so they were complacent (Rev. 3.15–17).

Complacency, apathy, and a lack of spiritual life are the leading causes of congregational plateauing. I believe Paul's encouragement to the Galatians applies here: "And let us not grow weary of doing good, for in due season we will reap, if we do not give up" (Gal. 6.9). The word rendered as "weary" is from *egkakomen,* the first-person plural present subjective of *egkakeo,* which can mean to be despondent, remiss, or faint-hearted.[15] Such *weariness* might lead to complacency, not because someone desires not to do what is good, but because he or she feels that where they are spiritually is satisfactory, even if that spirituality is mediocre and complacent.

By definition, congregational numerical plateauing implies an increase in spirituality and, so then, numbers that steadily climb for a certain amount of time. After a while, however, that increase in spirituality and attendance numbers begins to level off and renders the result of a numerical plateau. Notice I do not emphasize a decline in spirituality or numbers, for plateauing implies a sense of complacency and not a decline in spirituality. The plateaued congregation may have a commendable level of spirituality, but do not desire to change. They certainly do not want to decline, but they are afraid of improving if such improvement will involve the need to change.

Complacency and satisfaction with the present condition of a congregation arises from a number of circumstances:

1. The fear of change, as I addressed earlier. When a congregation is frightened of any sort of change, it will have

---

[15] To double check, I consulted *The Analytical Greek Lexicon Revised*, Harold K. Moulton, ed. (Grand Rapids, MI: Zondervan Publishing House, 1978), 112, 113 and *The New Analytical Greek Lexicon*, Wesley J. Perschbacher, ed. (Peabody, MA: Hendrickson Publishers, 1990), 113.

a tendency to desire to remain the same, change nothing, and be happy with where it is.
2. The attitude that if something appears to be going well, do not change course. Of course, change is also involved in this, but not in the same way as a fear of change. In this case, the desire not to change course or do anything different arises from two feelings:
   a. A sense of entitlement or satisfaction for what has been accomplished
   b. A lack of energy to do anything more or go any further
3. The belief that what got them where they are will always sustain them. This is similar to the statement, "If it ain't broke, don't fix it" (pardon the incorrect grammar). This attitude reflects a lack of desire to try to improve or refresh the planning and function of the congregation.

Servant leaders will address the reality of congregational numerical decline and plateauing by assessing their causes. If in their assessment they determine that the decline is due to expected, normal circumstances, such as individual and family relocation, then they must simply remain attuned to the pulse of the congregation to ascertain any future decline and the reasons for it. If it is determined that the decline is due to congregational malfunction, then proper steps must be taken to arrest it.[16]

If congregational numerical plateauing is determined, then servant leaders will seek to understand what is behind it. The leadership must determine the causes of the plateau and the congregation's attitude toward it. If the congregation is content with where they are, it is possible that no manner of vision casting or

---

[16] The former discussion of vision and implementation applies here.

statement of mission or strategic thinking will change their attitude, at least very much. Too often, when faced with the reality of numerical plateauing, the leadership will seek little more than a *Band-Aid* approach to altering the situation. In other words, good leaders will seek not to change the result (the plateauing itself), but the cause (complacency, misguided satisfaction, a lack of spiritual energy, or whatever).

Ineffective Elders' and Business Meetings

Allow me to briefly address one final issue in congregational leadership: the reality of ineffective elders' meetings and general congregational business meetings. In my opinion, the ability of the leadership to function effectively is greatly enhanced by the way they conduct their time while meeting. The elders of any congregation must realize who they are in the functioning of the congregation. Alexander Strauch comments, "Elders act as a body, a council, a team. As a team, they lead the church. A significant part of their work can be accomplished only by meeting together as a council."[17]

Elders' meetings[18] are often the *red-headed stepchild* of congregational leadership, especially in our busy, contemporary society. Too often, elderships treat their planned meetings as something to be done according to the dictates of their duties and as something to complete as quickly as possible. I am not saying that meetings cannot, at times, be routine, mundane, and even boring, depending on what needs to be discussed, and I am also not saying that time factors are not to be recognized and are not legitimate. The desire for short meeting times, however, is often reflective of the

---

[17] Strauch, *Meetings That Work*, 5.

[18] "Elders' meetings" is used a general way and would imply meetings that include only the elders or meetings that include the elders, deacons, preacher or staff, or any combination.

way those meetings are conducted. Details can be missed, information might be left out, and strategies may be restrained when meetings are set to stringent timetables and agendas.

I find such behavior and attitudes curious and puzzling. A significant purpose behind this book are the responsibilities of leadership that include the tasks of gathering of information, strategy and implementation, planning, assessment, and, as I will address in the next chapter, the inevitability of conflict and the need to find a resolution. No organization's leadership—political, business, military, or educational—can properly and effectively function without taking the time for collective thought and sharing. Of course, that also applies to the organization that is the congregation.

I believe the work of the eldership will improve in quality and effectiveness when a few simple things are observed. First, plan every meeting around prayer. It is a given that every eldership will begin and perhaps conclude their meetings with a prayer. Prayer, or reverence, however, must be the attitude that dominates what is done. It should not be only something spoken at a certain time, but such reverence and humility should dominate the meeting in its entirety. The apostles, when they commissioned the seven men for service, said that in continuing their duties, "we will give ourselves continually to prayer and to the ministry of the word" (Acts 6.4). Why should prayer dominate the meetings? The awesome task of shepherding the flock must be undertaken with hearts given to the omniscience and omnipotence of God. Paul did not encourage the church in Thessalonica to "Pray without ceasing" (1 Thes. 5.17) because he wished to constantly be saying a prayer. His intention was to encourage them to constantly be in the attitude of prayer. Given we are to be in such a constant attitude, how much more essential is it to be prayerful in the meetings of the shepherds of the church of God?

Second, establish and keep an agenda. Decide what is to be discussed and then stick with that agenda. Strauch comments, "A major cause of frustration with elders' meetings is the fact that no one takes responsibility to prepare for their success."[19] The point of an established agenda is that the meeting becomes focused and purposeful. Instead of, "Does anyone have anything to say?" the meeting carries with it a plan of discussion.

Third, communication prior to, during, and after the meeting is essential. I am a very staunch advocate of good communication in leadership concerns. Imagine how much time is lost in meetings when no one is familiar with information another has had for several days. An appeal for funding, a response to inquiries, or whatever has been sent to the eldership, which has been received and read only by one or two of the leaders. A portion of the meeting time is then taken up by acquainting the others regarding the contents of the communication. I suggest that in this day of email and cell phones, there is no reason communiqués cannot be shared and familiarized before a scheduled meeting commences.

Fourth, conduct the meetings in a secure and private location. This is another aspect of leadership I strongly advocate. Too often, elders' meetings are conducted in rooms that may be open to others passing by or nearby. Concern for eavesdropping, intentional or not, can stagnate and weaken effective, beneficial, and essential discussion. I believe it is vital that the eldership have a specific room, preferably laid out in the form of a boardroom, where business can be done without interruption and in private. In this room there should be a filing system of some kind: the standard file cabinet or computerized files. These files should contain materials and information pertinent to the meetings and the work of the leadership.

Fifth, emphasize ministry instead of the bottom-line. This, again, is another aspect of leadership I strongly advocate. I be-

---

[19] Strauch, *Meetings That Work*, 53.

lieve elderships across the nation spend too much time discussing the budget more than the spiritual matters of the congregation. I am not saying that budgetary concerns and financial stewardship are not essential and necessary tasks within the shepherding of the congregation. Indeed, they are. However, too often budgetary concerns and building and grounds maintenance consistently are the focus of elders' meetings. The elders should be able to have the time to carry out the duties Scripture allots them: acting as overseers, shepherds, and spiritual guardians (Acts 20.28–30; 1 Pet. 5.1–4); men of integrity, morality, honor, and maturity (2 Tim. 3.1–7); men who exhort and convict through a knowledge of the word (Titus 1.7–9).

When the elders of a congregation conduct their business in a productive and effective manner, their work can become more productive and effective. Part of that task is to establish and conduct meetings in an efficient manner so the maximum benefit can be realized.

EIGHT | *Conflict and Resolution*

Initially, I placed my research and writing about conflict and its resolution in chapter seven with "Issues of Leadership," but, as I worked deeper into the planning and formation of the book, I decided to devote an entire chapter to the topic. To be sure, the discussion of conflict and conflict resolution has a strong connection to the inevitability of change, for conflict is a typical byproduct of change, as well as the issues of power and values.[1]. Conflict and its resolution, however, also make a connection with the discussion of vision and implementation, as well as other issues of strategy and strategic thinking.

Thoughts on Conflict

Congregational conflict is an inevitable part of a congregation's existence, for it is improbable that a collection of individuals can exist, work, and function together without conflict. Roy Pneuman insisted that conflict is simply a part of everyday life.[2] In addition, congregational conflict is two-sided, for it can manifest itself into division and eventual disintegration or,

---

[1] Drury, *Handbook*, 70.

[2] Roy W. Pneuman, "Nine Common Sources of Conflict in Congregations," 4. The benefit of conflict an*d* its resolution will be discussed later.

if embraced and utilized properly, it can lead to positive development, reconciliation, and strength.

The question, then, is not whether conflicts will arise, but how those conflicts will be handled and managed. The choices are simple: congregations will handle and manage conflict in either healthy or unhealthy ways. Speed Leas emphasized the desire to seek mutually acceptable solutions, which are sought through the healthy process of cooperation rather than unhealthy competition. He insisted that healthy processes of resolution consider opposition and differences as valuable and informative.[3] Penny Becker, a Cornell University sociologist, insisted that conflict consists of several elements:[4]

1. Conflict is an intense form of sociation, or interaction. The opposite of conflict is not harmony but indifference or anonymity. To engage in conflict assumes a degree of connectedness between the parties.
2. Conflict involves two or more parties who perceive their interests to be incompatible and engage in action oriented to the defense of their interests.
3. Conflict is a pattern of interaction that is conscious, intermittent, and personal.

We are perhaps familiar with the phrase, "It takes two to tango." In the same way, a strong sense of interconnectedness, both positive and negative, is implied in an understanding of conflict. Also notice the implication of choice and decision within conflict. Each side will choose its perspective and then decide how to approach it as conflict intensifies. So then, as Dale wrote, "Conflict

---

[3] Speed B. Leas, "The Basics of Conflict Management in Congregations," in *Conflict Management in Congregations*, ed. David B. Lott (Bethesda, MD: The Alban Institute, 2001), 30–33.

[4] Penny Edgell Becker, *Congregations in Conflict: Cultural Models of Local Religious Life* (Cambridge, UK: Cambridge University Press, 1999). 37.

occurs when (1) two or more competitors (2) decide their goals and/or values can be attained by one side but not by both (3) and take overt action to reach their goals and/or values to the exclusion of others' goals and/or values."[5]

Hugh Halverstadt moved us even closer to the point when he wrote, "Conflicts are power struggles over differences."[6] Indeed, conflict is usually based on issues less critical to the bigger picture rather than things more pertinent to the whole. Perhaps more to the point is Shawchuck and Heuser's definition of conflict as issues of values and traditions, purposes and goals, and methods (actions). This moves us a bit closer to the crux of conflict, because so much of what we fight about involves our personal emotional property: traditions, goals, and methods.

Of course, the Bible is no stranger to conflict. Rome had congregational conflict (Rom. 12), as did Corinth (1 Cor. 1.11), and Ephesus (Eph. 4.1–6; 1 Tim. 5). James wrote to the scattered churches about favoritism (James 2), Peter wrote of submission (1 Pet. 3), and John warned Diotrophes of his desire for preeminence (3 Jn. 9–10). Conflict and the need for its resolution is nothing new and certainly is not isolated to any one congregation or even most congregations—it is a part of every congregation. As the congregations of the first-century church faced, embraced—and ideally, resolved—conflict, so should the congregations of today.

Conflict is feared because it is misunderstood and often mishandled. It is viewed as a sort of *Pandora's* Box—if someone does not open it, then it will not hurt us. Even though reasonable people know better, it is often believed that if conflict is left alone, it will eventually go away. Of course, that is rarely if ever true. The reality is that conflict is never to be left alone,

---

[5] Dale, *Pastoral Leadership*, 159.

[6] Hugh F. Halverstadt, *Managing Church Conflict* (Louisville, KY: Westminster/John Knox Press, 1991), 4.

for it signifies something much bigger that rests just under the surface. You see, conflict is a symptom and not a cause, and that is why it cannot be left alone.

Theological Reflection of Conflict Resolution

The Bible and the people and experiences within it are, of course, no stranger to conflict. Confrontations, clashes, personality differences, and literal battles are a constant thread throughout the biblical text and the story of God and His people. Examples would include:

- Lot's herdsman clashed with Abram's herdsmen, in spite of the latter's attempts to avoid conflict: "Let there be no strife between you and me, and between your herdsmen and my herdsmen…" (Gen. 13.8).
- Miriam and Aaron opposed the leadership of their young brother Moses (Num. 12.1–9).
- Absalom conspired against his father, King David, who was forced into exile (2 Sam. 15).
- Paul and Barnabas had "a sharp disagreement" over John Mark (Acts 15.36–41).

These and so many other examples of conflict within the biblical text provide ample evidence of conflict's place as well as its function, for the Bible does not hesitate to display such behavior within the human experience. Instead of ignoring or trying to explain away the existence of tension and conflict, the Bible puts it on display as a part of the reality of the story of God's people, for conflict is inevitable. The Bible does not only display the reality and inevitability of human conflict, but it provides the way such conflict is resolved.

Conflict resolution has a theological value, and that value can be seen in Romans twelve and fourteen to fifteen. Paul's examination of the Roman situation in chapters 1–11 becomes in this section a correction of their conflict. Chapters twelve through fifteen indicate three aspects of Paul's advice: (1) the proper Christian mind set (12.1–8), (2) the proper love for one another (12.9–21), and (3) an acceptance of one another through Jesus Christ (14.1–15.6).

The image of the sacrificial body is central to understanding and embracing a theology of human conflict and resolution. The body is to become a living sacrifice, one dedicated to the pursuit of righteousness.[7] Paul insisted that this sacrifice means that one is not conformed, but transformed through a renewal to what is good, acceptable, and complete.

The image in Romans 12 is of individual Christians, collectively presenting themselves as a corporate sacrifice (v. 1). Paul expanded on the image in the following verses by describing the individuals using their diverse gifts to build up a unified body.[8] Embedded in the sacrificial language is the example of humility and sacrifice set by Jesus (Phil. 2.8). With minds humbled through spiritual renewal, a sacrificial community becomes possible. Thus, if spiritual unity is to be achieved, Jesus must become the standard.[9]

The historical context from which Paul's words spring is the return of the Jews to Rome. James Walters reminded us that the expulsion also affected the Christian Jews in the city, evidenced

---

[7] Gerald Bray, ed. *Ancient Christian Commentary on Scripture: New Testament,* Vol. 6, "Romans" (Downers Grove, IL: InterVarsity Press, 1998), 305.

[8] James D.G. Dunn, "Romans 9–16," *Word Biblical Commentary,* Vol. 38 (Dallas: Word Books, 1988), 717. Dunn points out that Paul evidently found the body imagery to be effective encouragement, for it is found in 1 Corithians 12 and Ephesians 4 as well (733).

[9] R. Alan Culpepper, "God's Righteousness in the Life of His People: Romans 12–15," *Review and Expositor* 73 (Fall 1976): 453.

by the account of Aquila and Priscilla in Acts 18.2.[10] In the six years that followed the Jewish expulsion by Claudius in A.D. 49, the Gentile presence in the church in Rome became more dominant. Upon the return of the Christian Jews, tensions arose between them and their Gentile counterparts.

When the Christian Jews returned, they found it necessary to assert themselves. Dunn wrote, "They felt themselves doubly vulnerable as Jews, for they now had to identify themselves more fully with the largely Gentile 'church houses' in increasing distinction and separation from the synagogues."[11] Conflict arose between the Christian Jews and Gentiles not only due to the sense of superiority claimed by both sides, evidenced by Paul's response (chap. 2–11), but also in regard to a variety of cultural and religious practices (Romans 14–15).

Due to this tension, Paul wrote the epistle to encourage the Roman church toward love and harmony as a spiritual community.[12] Love in the community is movement toward one another, for it is movement in the same direction and with a common aim. Paul has the community evidently in mind in Romans 12, for he reintroduces the "one body in Christ" metaphor in verses 4–8, emphasizing a common good.[13] The Christian community is shaped by the desire for oneness with Christ. Clearly, this common aim is what makes the community distinctively Christian.[14]

[10] James Christopher Walters, *Ethnic Issues in Paul's Letter to the Romans: Changing the Self-Definitions in Earliest Roman Christianity*. Valley Forge, PA: Trinity Press International, 1993.

[11] Dunn, *Romans*, liii.

[12] Joseph Allen, "Renewal of the Christian Community: A Challenge for the Pastoral Community," *St. Vladimir's Theological Quarterly* 29 (January-March 1985): 308–309.

[13] Richard B. Hays, *The Moral Vision of the Testament: A Commentary Introduction to the New Testament Ethics* (San Francisco: Harper-Collins Publishers, 1996), 36.

[14] Allen, "Renewal of the Christian Community," 307.

Paul's instructions in verses 9–21 provides paraenetic[15] material intended to bring the Roman church in harmonious unity.[16] These verses instructed the Roman church about proper behavior. Building from the reality of one body, yet many members, functions, and gifts (3–8), Paul encouraged their sense of humility, which is a common theme within Paul's epistles.[17]

The tension within the congregation did not reflect a humble, sacrificial body. Therefore, said Paul, there are certain ethical issues to be considered. Paul insisted there is a place for both groups, and humility and sacrifice are the ways they will form a community.

Further Examination of Romans 12, 14–15

Romans 12.1–2. Paul opened up the discussion by getting to the crux of the matter, the spiritual mind and its function in the renewal of the Roman congregation. In this way, these verses serve as an introduction to 12.1–15.13, for all that follows illustrates and clarifies Paul's exhortation to bodies as a living sacrifice which forms the basis of renewal. As the "primary transitional link in the letter,"[18] verses 1–2 begin the discussion of what the Romans must do to achieve spiritual renewal as a Christian community through the resolution of conflict.

The immediate intent of the passage is two-fold: first, conformation versus transformation and second, the renewal of the

---

[15] This word refers to material that is meant to exhort, or to offer advice and counsel.

[16] N.T. Wright, *The New Testament and the People of God* (Minneapolis: Fortress Press, 1992), 362. Wright commented that ethical considerations were common in early Christian literature, not only in our text, but also in extra-biblical, non-inspired literature.

[17] Culpepper, "God's Righteousness," 453.

[18] Horace E. Stoessel, "Notes on Romans 12.1–2: The Renewal of the Mind and Internalizing the Truth," *Interpretation* 17 (April 1963): 161.

mind, which indicates that transformation comes through a renewal of the mind. Paul encouraged the Romans not to choose conformation, which is of the world, but transformation through the renewal of the mind, which is union with God.

We can agree with Luther's interpretation of Paul's sense of transformation as the act of becoming better and, so, being good.[19] This view emphasizes the process of spiritual growth that can only come when one rejects what is in the world. It turns us away from the effects of the world and causes us to respond in faith, hope, and love to the unconditional love and mercy God has for us.

The transformation Paul speaks of indicates a continual process, reminiscent of Paul's words elsewhere: "inwardly we are being renewed day by day" (2 Cor. 4.16). What does this mean? Consider that "the act of baptism implies redemption that, in turn, implies freedom and it is freedom that exemplifies, in part, transformation."[20] Freedom is expressed in the concept of transformation, for renewal implies a rejection of the world, so then freedom from it. Transformation as freedom is a theological point of the church, for it reveals a changed (renewed) and gathered people brought out of the slavery of sin into the light (freedom) that illuminates them as belonging to God. In this way we see how Paul implies the sense of community in the concept of transformation. This community is formed by those who are gathered through the renewal of minds given to God.

Paul's emphasis is on the individual mind, for Paul never uses the plural form of *nous* (mind), which is a collective noun that

---

[19] Martin Luther, *Commentary on the Epistle to the Romans*, trans. J. Theodore Mueller (Grand Rapids, MI: Kregel Publications, 1976), 167–168.

[20] Vigen Guroian, "Seeing Worship as Ethics: An Orthodox Perspective," *Journal of Religious Ethics* 13 (Fall 1995): 340.

indicates Paul speaks to "individuals in their solidarity."[21] Paul implies a Christological point. The concept of *nous* as applied to thinking the same thing (community thinking) is a theology of Christ.[22] Paul often thought of Jesus as the suffering servant (cf. Rom. 4.25; 5.19; 2 Cor. 5.21).[23]

Horace Stoessel rejects a view of *nous* that refers to what is common in all men, the rational faculty. He insisted that such is only a partial explanation, for with Paul *nous* is never simply "reason," but intelligibility rather than mere reason and edification. Rationality alone is not all Paul has in mind.[24] While "reason" might be a legitimate translation of *nous*, it is perhaps better translated as part of "moral reason," for Paul's usage here has strong ethical overtones, as elsewhere (cf. Rom. 1.28; Eph. 4.17ff; 1 Tim. 6.5; 2 Tim. 3.8). The use of *nous* also involves an objective aspect, indicating an external standard, "the ideas and principles which are the springs of action."[25]

These concerns are Christological. When Paul called for a renewal of mind, he referred less to reason than to the revitalization of the church's theological foundation of the individual, spiritual mind and the attitude, viewpoint, or understanding nurtured by it.[26] How is this done? Paul does not offer a clear answer but appears to emphasize the place and function of mind-renewal. Stoessel wrote that "Romans abounds in clues suggesting what mind-renewal includes," and offered four suggestions of the in-

---

[21] Stoessel, "Romans 12.1–2," 162–163.

[22] Ibid., 166.

[23] Walter A. Elwell, ed. *The Concise Evangelical Dictionary of Theology* (Grand Rapids, MI: Baker Book House, 1991), 94.

[24] Stoessel, Romans 12.1–2," 163–164. He cited 1 Cor. 1.10, Rom. 7.23, 25, and Romans 14.5 as examples.

[25] Ibid., 164.

[26] Ibid., 167.

dividual's role in mind-renewal: (1) mind-renewal proceeds under the guidance and power of the spirit with prayers and submissions, (2) mind-renewal occurs within the community of believers, not as a private transaction, (3) mind-renewal is a continuing process, and (4) mind-renewal must lead to practical actions, indicated by Paul's words, "That you may prove…" (12.2).[27]

Romans 12.3–8. Having established the foundation of a spiritual community, transformation through a renewed mind, Paul shifts his thinking to issues of practice (praxis). While it is generally agreed that Paul's paraenetic (exhortation; advice and counsel) material is found in verses 9–21, we find ethical instructions beginning in verse three. These ethical considerations reemphasize our prior discussion of *nous* and the individual mind that is formed in solidarity. Vigen Guroian correctly stated, "There is no such thing as a Christian ethic which is exclusive of a single individual. Apart from the Church there is no Christian ethic."[28] This section of the text closely resembles 1 Corinthians 12. Paul exhorts humility and unity. No room for pride. No provision for second-class membership in the body.[29] It is community, unity in diversity. How does a transformed community live with diversity? There is value in diversity. Christian community becomes an example of the living body and a lack of community is a failure in recreating that body.[30]

Failure to be a community comes from three causes. First, the aim of the community can fail if the living body fails to be precisely a body, i.e. visible and incarnate in the world. The unity in

---

[27] Ibid.

[28] Guroian, "Seeing Worship as Ethics," 353.

[29] Culpepper, "God Righteousness," 453.

[30] Joseph Allen, "Renewal of the Christian Community: A Challenge for the Pastoral Ministry," *St. Vladamir's Theological Quarterly* 29 (Nov-Dec 1985): 305–323..

diversity becomes a facet of this community. Second, the community fails because of a lack of forgiveness, yet community is the place of forgiveness.[31] Third, the community fails if there is no humility. Community is not where people live nor a work team, but a place where people emerge from the shadows of egocentricity into the light of real love.[32]

Paul's words are reflective of a biblical portrait of the components of spiritual community and, therefore, of conflict resolution. Several key components are found in the Pauline epistles and elsewhere in the New Testament.

- **Humility**: humility that comes from wisdom (James 3.13); clothing ourselves in humility (1 Pet. 5.5)
- **Sacrifice**: Jesus was presented as a sacrifice (Rom. 3.25); Jesus was a fragrant offering and sacrifice (Heb. 9.26); we are made holy through the sacrifice of Jesus (Heb. 10.10, 14); Jesus is the atoning sacrifice for sins (1 John 2.2; 4.10)
- **Prayer**: all joined together in prayer (Acts 1.14); they engaged in the breaking of bread and prayer (Acts 2.42); Paul was helped by Corinth's prayers (2 Cor. 1.11); prayer is part of the armor of God (Eph. 6.18)
- **Giftedness**: how God has gifted us will form a unity and these gifts serve, not cancel, a transformed community; Paul instructed Timothy not to neglect his gift (1 Tim. 4.14); Paul instructed Timothy to fan the gift of God (2 Tim. 1.6); Peter encouraged the scattered churches to use their gifts to serve others (1 Pet. 4.10); Paul connected the gifts to the body (1 Cor. 12); Paul encouraged Corinth to eagerly desire the spiritual gifts

---

[31] Allen, "Renewal," 312.
[32] Ibid., 313.

Community renewal, then, must belong to God and becomes God's work of renewal and is *pneumatological*[33] activity, leading to an *eschatological*[34] reality.[35] The faithful are drawn into their baptismal life of dying and rising with Christ, and such newness is distinctly eschatological.[36] George Ladd wrote that central to Paul's eschatology is consummation.[37] "Community" is at stake, and Romans 12 falls between specific problems in 9.1–11.12 and tensions in 14.1–15.6.[38]

The composition of Romans 12.3–8 is connected to specific circumstances that lead to community thinking and the unity of the body, such as *nous*, which implies community thinking and is a theology of Christ from pre-existence to ministry to trial and death to resurrection (Phil. 2.5ff). Such is no empty creed, insisted Stoessel, but a living truth that determines community attitudes (cf. Rom. 12.16).[39]

Romans 12.9–21; 14–15. Having laid the groundwork for spiritual community, unity, and love within the congregation in Rome, Paul then makes some summary statements in vv. 9–21 and some situational statements in chapters 14–15. So, having laid the groundwork of conflict and its resolution, I will briefly observe the information offered in each section of the texts.

Culpepper wrote that at this point in the epistle to the Romans, the text changes from humility and unity to genuine love

---

[33] This word refers to the study of the Holy Spirit.

[34] This word refers to the study of the "last days," and so the second coming of Jesus Christ.

[35] Allen, "Renewal," 315–316.

[36] George Eldon Ladd,, *A Theology of the New Testament* (Grand Rapids, MI: William B. Eerdmans Publishing Company, 1974), 479.

[37] Ibid., 552.

[38] David Alan Black, "The Pauline Love Command: Structure, Style, and Ethics in Romans 12.9–21," *Filologia Neotestamentaria* 2 (May 1989): 14.

[39] Stoessel, "Romans 12.1–2," 166.

and a response to God's grace.[40] Yet these things seem to be interconnected, humility and unity through genuine love. These are communal statements. Relationality becomes central to how such love is expressed and practiced. The theological heart is found here, from which a strategy is formed. We need to form a strategy for conflict resolution because God has brought us to peace. According to Paul, such a strategy is founded upon a genuine love (9) that seeks to "love one another with brotherly affection" (10). Such brotherly love (Greek, *philadephia*) and devotion (*philostorgoi*) is demonstrated by their willingness to "outdo" (ESV) or "giving preference" (NKJV) to each other in showing honor, never being slothful in their zeal (*spoude*), which seems to be connected to the command to "contribute" (ESV) or "share" (NKJV), from *oinovountes*, in showing hospitality (*philoxenian*).

While it can be argued that Paul's material often contained things common to his teaching to all the churches, 12.9–21 appears to address a situation peculiar to Rome. It very well may be that the persecution Paul wrote about (14) was not from outside antagonists, but "in house," which may be further explained in vv. 17–21.[41] If so, their behavior toward one another was reprehensible and offers some insight into Paul's motivation to encourage their resolution of such conflict. Culpepper saw an echo of Jesus' own words in Mt. 5.38–42 and Luke 6.29, as well as Jesus' use of "peacemakers" (Mt. 5.9) and loving one's enemies (Mt. 5.44).

Chapters 14–15 are less paraenetic, and specifically address the particular situation in Rome. More specifically, Paul in this section may have Rome in mind, along with Corinth (cf. Rom. 14.1–15.13 to 1 Cor. 8 and 10) and Jerusalem, where he had decided to return to promote unity (15.25). So then, chapters 14–15

---

[40] Culpepper, "God's Righteousness," 453.

[41] Black, "Pauline Love Command," 10.

are in regard to the struggles and behaviors of weak Christians. The material can be divided into three sections:

- 14.1–12 is about the weak
- 14.13–23 is about the strong
- 15.1–13 calls for the strong to imitate the example of Jesus Christ

Even though the strong are emphasized, Paul instructed each group to accept one another. So then, the strong must accept the weak because God has accepted them. At the same time, the weak should not judge the strong. The emphasis for both groups is to avoid pride in righteousness, hence the apostle's reminder that the kingdom is a kingdom of righteousness, peace, and joy rather than food and drink (14.17).

In 15.1–6, Paul reemphasizes his former instructions, information, and rebuke. He uses *oikodomen*, "to build up," in 15.2 as well as 14.19, and both may stress corporate (community; body) edification. Verses 5–6 encourage conflict resolution through emphasis on harmonious living and the intent to build a community of unity and oneness. The reality illuminated in 12.1–8 produces the need for and practice of conflict resolution in 15.5–6.

Observations About Conflict Resolution

Leaders will do themselves a favor if they construct ways to keep their fingers on the pulse of their congregations, finding ways to measure the emotions and eruptions that occur from time-to-time. An elder of a very large congregation once told me that shepherding that congregation was little more than constantly putting out *fires*. He was using the word *fires* to indicate little problems here and there. That eldership would be much better off to locate the source(s) of the *fires* and then remove it/them rather than to run from flame to flame.

There is, of course, the opposite side to this. Just as it is common for elderships to do too little in regard to conflict, it is also true that some tend to do too much. They desire to arbitrate every squabble and referee every disagreement. Of course, such a desire is not practical or even possible. Leaders who try to do this usually end up micro-managing everything to the point of no productivity. Tension is added to the general atmosphere of the congregation because of such micro-management, and that tension leads to greater conflict. Effective leaders will seek a balance between what is to be managed and what is best left alone. As we will discuss later, there is a benefit to allowing conflict to occur and even, in limited circumstances, to run its course. There are no simple guidelines on doing this efficiently, because each congregation is different. Each individual set of leaders must decide if, when, where, and how to address issues of conflict.

Conflict ————→ Tension ——————→ Greater Conflict

Conflict is often avoided because of some preconceived notion of how a congregation is supposed to look and supposed to do. Dale commented that conflict "surprises and disappoints many church members…because we view congregations idealistically. We want the body of Christ to be a perfect community."[42] To most people, conflict only indicates problems and a potential negative result, which often becomes reality because conflict is left unmanaged or poorly led, and is allowed to infect the minds of those it touches.

Why do conflicts occur within a community of faith? Of course, the answers are legion, too numerous to list in this study. Dale puts it more simply by offering six perspectives of congregational conflict:[43]

---

[42] Dale, *Pastoral Leadership*, 159.

[43] Ibid., 91.

1. Conflict generally indicates a relationship. We rarely waste energy by fussing with strangers.
2. Conflict among friends or acquaintances is especially threatening. After all, the relationship is at stake. And, people who know each other well also know how to cause maximum hurt with minimum effort.
3. When people feel strongly about an issue, their conflicts tend to be heavily emotionally laden.
4. Group conflict produces conflict that polarizes and moralizes.
5. Healthy congregations settle their differences promptly. By dealing with their conflicts more often, they use their ongoing experiences to learn how to resolve their fusses more constructively.
6. Suppressing conflict often leads to explosions.

Dale identifies one of the most common sources of congregational conflict in the first two perspectives: relationships. The church is an *ekklesia*, a called-out community and a community of faith and commitment. Therefore, by definition and function, congregations are communities of relationships, and as a community, those relationships play a major role in whatever is done. An old song stated that you always hurt the ones you love. In all of the preaching and teaching about congregations being *family* and acting like a *family*, the one way they often reveal the existence of *family* is by squabbling and arguing like a family.

As spiritual communities and families, congregations are filled to the brim with people who know each other all too well. Too often they know the tender spots of another's emotions, the darker secrets of another, the issues of their fleshly families, the mistakes, quirks, and inconsistencies. Such relationships are filled with those who know how to hurt one another the most in the least amount of time. Knowing when to step in and when to step back is part of the task of leaders in times of conflict.

Dale also identifies legitimate elements of conflict in perspectives number three, four, and five: differences and commitments. Everyone has an opinion and some hold to their opinions rather fondly, tending to become irate when their views are threatened, questioned, or ignored. Shawchuck and Heuser wrote, "Feelings and emotions often are much more powerful than thought or reason in ecclesiastical disputes. We might wish it otherwise, but it is not."[44] We all know this is true, for we have seen it erupt in business meetings and elders' meetings for decades: the controversies often arise over opinions rather than facts. Dale differentiated between conflicts over facts and conflicts over feelings, insisting that each have their own substance and must be managed accordingly and appropriately.[45]

Often conflicts over feelings and opinions arise because it is believed that someone must be wrong and someone must be right. However, it is entirely possible that two people with differing views can be right or, at least, offer legitimate thoughts. Three things might be observed from this:

1. Even though two people may seem to offer differing positions, they both may offer a valid perspective to the discussion. This is where good leaders will become good arbitrators and negotiators. They will seek to find a way to blend the two perspectives so that both opinions are honored.
2. Two people with seemingly differing opinions may be saying the same thing, only in different ways. Good leaders will find the core thought in someone's opinion. He or she may not express themselves very well, but may have something legitimate to offer.

---

[44] Shawchuck and Heuser, *Managing*, 251.

[45] Dale, *Pastoral Leadership*, 159ff.

3. Differences of opinions may be little more than personality issues. Some people like to disagree or be negative in their thinking. Perhaps we all have heard the story of the deacon running into a meeting one night. When he arrived, the rest of the deacons were in heated discussion over an issue unknown to the newcomer. Nonetheless, at his first opportunity, he spoke up: "I don't what you are talking about and I don't know what you have decided, but whatever it is, I am against it." Good leaders will try to see the personalities behind differing opinions.

Finally, Dale brings up a very valid point in the sixth and last perspective: suppressing conflict is dangerous. Sometimes, it is necessary to just let conflict rise and take its course. Shakespeare addresses this in his play *King John* when he writes, "So foul a sky clears not without a storm." Think of phrases such as "get it out into the open," "lay your cards on the table," or "clearing the air," and their implications of allowing things to be said and done that might be beneficial in getting to the bottom of an issue or dispute.

The key to this is not the conflict itself, but how that conflict is managed. Marriage counselors will sometimes just allow the couple they are counseling to express themselves, even if their argument becomes heated. In this way, the counselor can hear what is really going on inside the issue without any attempt to soften or deflate the emotions involved.

Leaders who have difficulty with control issues might find doing this hard because they feel when an argument ensues, they are no longer in control. Think of what foresters will do during a "controlled burn" of forested or grass-covered land. They will purposefully ignite timber, brush, and grasses on fire and step back and watch the fire's progress. They are allowing what appears to be destructive activity to occur, but they are in control of the fire every step of the way. They also know that what appears to be destructive is actually beneficial. Leaders who are *rescuers* or *helpers* in personality might have trouble allowing an argument to occur. They might feel intimidated by the conflict and tension, and feel nothing productive can come when two people argue. To them, it is only an amount of time before real problems begin; nothing good can come of this, they believe.

The key to allowing conflict to occur and not suppressing it is placing that conflict and tension in a controlled environment. In these events, leaders will become listeners. They will allow the emotions to arise so that true feelings and frustrations can be vented. They will act as the release-valve for those emotions and when the emotions are spent and feelings are expressed, they then will become arbitrators, unpacking the argument so that all can see what has occurred. They will also become negotiators seeking to find common ground and similarities.

The bottom-line is that conflict must be managed and resolved. Shawchuck and Heuser write, "Whatever the source of the conflict, if it is not managed, it will soon take root in one of three dimensions," which they list in order of their difficulty.[46] The first dimension they list is conflict over values and traditions and is, according to them, the most difficult to manage. I mentioned in chapter six the issue of generational differences, and it is in regard to values and traditions that those differences might be best seen. Often these differences arise in relation to youth groups and youth-oriented events. The *Silent Generation* (48–63 in 1993) in a given congregation probably has a different set of values and traditions than *Generation X* (1–28 in 1993), and the *Boomer Generation* (29–47 in 1993) probably has different values and traditions than the *G.I. Generation* (64–92 in 1993). Put simply, each generation will perhaps do things differently, think

---

[46] Shawchuck and Heuser, *Managing the Congregation*, 257.

differently, and place value on things differently, and that can cause traumatic conflict.

The problem in values-traditions conflict is that compromise is extremely difficult. As Shawchuck and Heuser put it, "if you compromise on a value, then it is no longer (for you) a value."[47] Very recently, I read the contributions to a discussion on whether wearing suits and ties to a worship service was necessary. The discussion followed generational lines: those of the *Silent Generation* believed it was (it is a matter of decency and order), while those of *Generation X* did not (it is about what is in your heart), and those among the *Boomer Generation* either took one view or the other, or were completely neutral.

One way for leaders to manage such conflict is to redirect those involved toward a higher value that can be agreed upon, causing the values demanded before to be replaced by something greater (more valuable). In addition, the leaders might challenge those involved to adopt the values of the others for a period of time (role-play, perhaps) to see what it is like to live and think in such a value system. Sometimes, values-traditions conflict arises only because one generation or one *side* does not understand what it means for the other to feel as they do or hold the values they do.

A second dimension of conflict, according to Shawchuck and Heuser, is conflict over purpose and goals, which they claim is the second most difficult to manage. They define goals as "desired future conditions that grow out of our sense of values and our mission, which are highly influenced by our traditions and boundaries."[48] This takes us back to our discussion of vision and mission in chapter four and the need to express them effectively so all can embrace the goals they contain. Conflict arises when

---

[47] Shawchuck and Heuser, *Managing the Congregation*, 258

[48] Ibid.

some are not able to embrace the goals as stated, feeling that another goal or set of goals is more desirable.

In every instance of conflict over purpose and goals, there is always one individual or small group who arise as the antagonists of the conflict. Based on their values and traditions, they see the goals of the congregation in a certain way. They often fail, even refuse, to see things any other way. This is why leaders must express the vision and mission of the congregation clearly enough so that all involved can embrace it. Anyone who has had to pitch a sales, production, or manufacturing idea to a governing board will understand how essential it is to explain the concept well enough that all will understand it. The bottom-line is if they do not understand it, they will not embrace it. The same can be said in congregational conflict over purpose and goals: if it is not understood, it will not be accepted and so conflict arises.

Dale wrote:

> churches have two kinds of goals—even if they don't deliberately set goals. Survival and mission goals characterize most congregations. Survival goals usually involve bodies (membership growth), budgets, and buildings. Concentrating on these survival-motivated goals turns congregations inward. Mission goals turn congregations outward and press them to clarify their unique identities, ministry directions, and community opportunities.[49]

While there are perhaps other purposes and goals, Dale offered a valid foundation of potential conflict. How many congregational business meetings, elders' and deacons' meetings, or elders' meetings become bogged down due to disagreement over whether to build up the weekly contribution or finance a particular evangelistic effort? On one side, it is the goal of proper

---

[49] Dale, *Pastoral Leadership*, 87.

stewardship, while on the other side, it is the goal of the Great Commission (cf. Mt. 28.18–20).

Once again, such conflict is difficult to resolve, but it is not something insurmountable. Compromise may be a key factor here. I do not refer to compromise as a disposal of values, and certainly not as a lessening of biblical doctrine. Compromise, in this case, is finding common ground without one or both sides losing the values they hold dear. Yet, common ground is there and must be claimed if resolution is to be done. When survival and mission are antagonistic goals and purposes, the biblical command of evangelism is possible common ground. Working within the vision of the congregation, the two sides can find a way to evangelize the community while being good stewards of the church's resources.

The third dimension of conflict, according to Shawchuck and Heuser, is conflict over methods, which they insist is the third most difficult type of conflict to manage. They define methods as "the actions that the congregation takes to achieve its goals."[50] Put simply, this is conflict over how things get done, whether it is the way the preacher preaches, the way an eldership handles a problem, the order and practice of a worship service, the format of Vacation Bible School, how visitors' cards are to distributed and collected, or another procedural issue.

This a change issue, to be sure. Becker did a study of twenty-three congregations and arrived at a central, core concept: "congregations develop distinct cultures that comprise local understandings of identity and mission and that can be understood analytically as bundles of core tasks and legitimate ways of doing things."[51] Put more simply, she found that every congregation developed a certain way of doing things that was understood in that congregation. Consequently, when anyone (new or other-

---

[50] Shawchuck and Heuser, *Managing the Congregation*, 259.

[51] Becker, *Congregations in Conflict*, 12ff.

wise) would propose changes to the way things were done, conflict arose. Such conflict often bogs down in the mire between comfort (that is how it has always been done) and effectiveness/efficiency (this way is best). Conflict like this becomes an issue of change: we once did it this way but now we will do it that way. The leaders during this sort of conflict must be able to differentiate between change for the sake of change and change for the sake of efficiency: should certain methods be adopted because they are new or because they will be better? Leaders must also be able to decide when an issue of method becomes one of nostalgia/tradition versus an attempt to try something new. Each of these issues—changes for change's sake, tradition/nostalgia, efficiency, and newness—have their own merit and must be properly considered as the conflict is resolved.

There is also an unfortunate reality to congregational conflict that has little or nothing to do with personalities, emotions, feelings, opinions, traditions, or generations. It is what Shawchuck and Heuser calls "unvarnished human cussedness [and] sinful cantankerousness," adding, "what a cruel treachery Christians visit upon one another."[52] My father, a gospel preacher for a half century, told me when I was a young, green, wet-behind-the-ears preacher that I will never be treated better and I will never be treated worse than by the brethren. Unfortunately, that was sage wisdom from a very intelligent man. The brutal truth is that conflict sometimes arises because some people are cruel and mean-spirited.

This unfortunate circumstance manifests itself in a variety of ways. It might be the elder or member that seeks to dominate and control, even to the point of manipulation and coercion. Diotrophes, who desired the preeminence, would be an example of this (3 Jn. 9–10). It might be the member or members who take

---

[52] Shawchuck and Heuser, *Managing the Congregation*, 251.

pleasure in spreading rumor, innuendo, and gossip throughout the congregation, regardless of who they might hurt. Paul spoke of some young widows who had learned to be idle, "wandering about from house to house, and not only idle but gossips and busybodies, saying things which they ought not" (1 Tim. 5.13).

Regardless of the type of individual, these circumstances obviously force conflict to the surface, and few, if any, congregations are immune to such behavior. Good leaders will—indeed, they must—put a stop to it immediately, as is their prerogative and authority (Acts 20.28–30; 1 Tim. 3.5; Titus 1.9; 1 Pet. 5.1–4). Unfortunately, such behavior goes unchecked and unquestioned all too often. Of all the issues of conflict I have mentioned, I believe this to be the most difficult to manage, because nothing that is mean-spirited has any place within the spiritual community of the church and yet it is there all too often. So in spite of its obvious malevolence and lack of any redeeming or meritorious worth, it exists in the darker places of the congregation and has the potential to cause serious and sometimes irreparable harm.

Conflict and its resolution is an inevitable task of leadership. It emerges due to issues of change, personalities, ideologies, doctrinal differences, and, unfortunately, mean-spirited behavior. The challenge must be met head on so the congregation can move beyond the conflict and even benefit from it.

Conclusion

So much more could be said regarding congregational and spiritual leadership. The task is essential to the spiritual health of every congregation, for without it, congregations would drift and waver, and potentially collapse. Even congregations that do not have elders must develop effective leadership.[1] It is the opinion of this writer that the servant leader model is an effective way of doing congregational and ministry leadership. It is best represented through foundational and functional components that seek to be transformational, that emerge from leaders who seek authenticity and are oriented around the servant-follower relationship and team work.

By *servant leadership*, I do not focus on the model proposed by Greenleaf in the 1970s, even though his idea of the methodology has much to offer: not a leader-centric model, but one that emphasized the leader as a servant to the organization he or she serves. His focus on transformational and authentic leadership with the centricity of the leader-follower relationship made Greenleaf's proposal very appealing. The servant leader model

---

[1] I do not address leadership in congregations with no elders in this book. I debated with myself whether to include it or not, and decided to leave it for another time. While some of the issues, methodologies, and practical aspects of leadership apply, there are several other concerns that must be discussed in this context. Vision casting and a statement of mission, strategic concerns, conflict resolution and change, and the leader-follower relationship take on a different perspective when there are no elders.

that I am proposing for congregational shepherds takes the foundational elements of Greenleaf's model just mentioned and then folds in the biblical expectations of transformation, humility, maturity, stewardship, responsibility, faith, and spirituality.

Over the past few decades, several social and communicative concerns were introduced into the research to determine how they address a variety of cooperative issues that may or may not have been avoided in former leader-centric studies. Within this research also emerged a conscious appraisal of the moral component of leadership, especially within the transformational and authentic leadership models. Out of this school of thought has come a greater awareness of the leader as a servant to those he leads.

While the research and assessment of the servant leadership model is still relatively young, I believe it is a viable, effective model of leadership within a congregational setting. My intention in advocating the servant leadership model is not to imply that no other model of leadership is viable—that is not the case. In the environment of the congregation, however, the servant leader model perhaps fits best because of the servant grid that is laid over the task of leading and managing:

- Casting a vision as servants of the congregation, with an emphasis on the whole rather than the few
- A statement and implementation of the mission as servants in a way that best utilizes the congregation's resources (physical and human) in a realistic and effective way that is transformational
- A desire to address change and resolve conflict in a way that stresses the spiritual development of the congregation rather than a temporary fix

The idea of servant leadership is supported biblically, to be sure, for the Godly leaders described within it were servants to those they led. The stories of Moses and the Exodus, Nehemiah and rebuilding the walls of Jerusalem, Paul and his guidance for and example of leadership, and so many others, cry out the demands of leaders who would also be servants. Jesus is, of course, the best example of what servant leadership is intended to be, displayed perhaps most effectively, first, in His washing of the disciples' feet (Jn. 13.1–20) and, second and foremost, in His sacrifice on the cross (Mt. 27; Mark 15; Luke 23; John 19).

The leadership within every congregation must have one focus: Jesus Christ and His church, certainly an emphasis within the framework of servant leadership. All else falls under that focus point: vision and mission, strategy, and managing the congregation through the issues that arise. With Jesus Christ as the focus, then Christ-likeness will become the manner in which leadership is done. Congregational leadership is not a power-trip or a quest for control, but the release of all rights to power and control, giving it all to Jesus Christ, where it belongs. Congregational leaders are to be servant-leaders, serving first the Lord who redeemed them, then serving the congregation they shepherd, and finally, serving each other within the leadership.

Congregational leaders are to be a power force of vision and mission, defining who the congregation will be and what it will do. Congregational leaders are strategists, agents of scriptural change, equippers, agents of empowerment, motivators, listeners, facilitators, arbitrators, negotiators, and builders. As a chain is only as strong as its weakest link, the congregation will never be stronger and more faithful than its leaders. That is why congregational leadership must be strong in faith, commitment, and spirit, striving to grow as disciples of the Lord.

The task of the eldership is a good work, according to Paul (1 Tim. 3.1). Those who function under the shepherding and authority of the eldership—deacons, ministry staff, teachers, and worship leaders—implement the vision and mission the elders have established for the congregation. That is why congregational leadership is an awesome as well as a daunting task; it requires maturity, integrity, knowledge, commitment, and, of course, a lot of prayer. Congregational shepherds epitomize the essence of the Shepherd of Psalm 23, and exemplify the character and qualifications expected of them (cf. Acts 20.17–35; 1 Tim. 3.1–7; Titus 1.5–9; et al.). They shoulder the spiritual future of the congregation they serve. They are the target of the critics but rarely the recipients of support, and especially praise.

Congregational shepherds are leaders who are servants. God bless those who lead our congregations.

APPENDIX | *A Church Growth Program*

One+Plus+One: Adding To The Church One Person At A Time

Introduction

Numerical and spiritual church growth is the intended goal of every congregation, but is often difficult to achieve. A variety of methodologies are attempted, too often with little or no positive results. Why is this? Certainly not for a lack of trying, nor a lack of desire, to be sure, trying methods ranging from door-to-door, "leafleting," the mass mailing of *House-to-House,* and radio and TV broadcasts. These are all legitimate, effective, proven methods that vary in effectiveness depending on the era of time, personnel, planning, and, of course, money.

In our modern internet/social media times, going door-to-door is limited due to a loss of face-to-face community—a knock on the door may or may not be as welcome as it once was; it looks too much like the Mormons and Jehovah's Witnesses. Leafleting has its problems in a day when junk mail is so prevalent. Radio and television can be very effective because they touch people through high-tech—which is an appeal in this computer/internet/social media age—and do not invade an individual's sense of privacy, as does a knock on the door. Cost-effectiveness is a concern, however, because radio is somewhat costly and television certainly is.

So, what are we do to evangelize, to engage in effective numerical and spiritual growth within the Lord's church?

The Biblical Mandate of Evangelism

It is obvious that we are to evangelize. Matthew 28.18–20 establishes that very clearly: "Go therefore and make disciples of all nations, baptizing them in] the name of the Father and of the Son and of the Holy Spirit, teaching them to observe all that I have commanded you. And behold, I am with you always, to the end of the age." The Book of Acts (The Acts of the Apostles) is an account of the first three-and-one-half decades of the church and major element of that account is the act of evangelism: Pentecost (chapter 2), Philip and the Ethiopian (8), Lydia, as well as the Philippian jailer (16), at least four Areopagites (17), and so on.

Jesus said to his disciples, "The harvest is plentiful, but the laborers are few; therefore pray earnestly to the Lord of the harvest to send out laborers into his harvest" (Matt. 9.37–38). We must be people who go out into the harvest of the Lord, so then we must become evangelistic people, revealing the gift of Jesus' death (cf. Rom. 5.8; et al.) and the scheme of redemption (cf. Acts 2.38; et al.).

Paul wrote in 1 Corinthians 5.17–21:

> Therefore, if anyone is in Christ, he is a new creation; the old has gone, the new has come! All this is from God, who reconciled us to himself through Christ and gave us the ministry of reconciliation: that God was reconciling the world to himself in Christ, not counting men's sins against them. And he has committed to us the message of reconciliation. We are therefore Christ's ambassadors, as though God were making his appeal through us. We implore you on Christ's behalf: Be reconciled to

God. God made him who had no sin to be sin for us, so that in him we might become the righteousness of God.

The passage refers to "anyone" who is in Christ, which includes everyone who is in Christ. Paul explained that God gave all of us the "ministry of reconciliation," for He has "committed to us the message of reconciliation." He concluded, "We are therefore Christ's ambassadors," so God is "making His appeal through us." God's commission to us, then, concludes for God with the declaration, "...in Him we might become the righteousness of God."

When combined with such concepts as our being "the light of the world" and "the salt of the earth," it would seem to me that the above passage, while it is probably being applied specifically to the Apostles in this case, applies to all of us generally as well.

The Model of One+Plus+One

While biblical evangelism often focused on the missionary journey or the chance meeting, ONE+PLUS+ONE is biblical in concept. In Acts 2.42–47, we are told that following the baptism of three-thousand souls on the day of Pentecost, "they devoted themselves to the apostles' teaching and the fellowship, to the breaking of bread and prayers." The text continues to speak of their fellowship and shared devotion, having all things in common, and their practice of "praising God and having favor with all the people." The result was that "the Lord added to their number day by day those who being saved." What is implied, in part, in this text is the development of relationships with those around them, or the enhancement of relationships already in place, and how such fellowship and devotion brought others into the Lord's church.

ONE+PLUS+ONE is simple in its design, but potentially effective in its implementation. It works from the idea of what has been called "friendship evangelism" or "contagious Christianity," that we can add to the Lord's church by evangelizing our friends, family, and acquaintances. Its implementation is simple. Each family of the church chooses one person to encourage in any given year—just one. Then, through friendship, encouragement, and Bible study, that one would be led toward becoming a Christian according to the standards and commands of the New Testament. Instead of giving the church high(er) figures of souls being added to the church ("We want to add thirty new people to the church in 20??"), each family is responsible for one. Of course, if a family brings someone to the Lord, let's say in April of a given year, they can and should set their sights on one more.

What does this look like spiritually and numerically? Spiritually, it can bring a new level of faith and practice into the congregation because each family is taking some ownership of the evangelistic goals. Such participation makes each family a part of the future of the congregation, eliminating more of the so-called "fringe" within each congregation ("fringe" is defined as those who attend sporadically, usually only on Sunday morning and usually only for worship, and do little or nothing involving the work of the congregation). Numerically, ONE+PLUS+ONE offers the potential for substantial growth. Let's say a given congregation has forty families (including individuals). Common statistical estimates indicate the average congregation can expect fifty to sixty percent participation at first with any new program or project of work. (NOTE: as the program/project proves successful, the percentage of participation normally increases somewhat). Let's take the conservative figure of fifty percent, meaning that twenty families/individuals will seek one person to add to the Yucaipa congregation in 2015. If fifty percent of those twenty families are able to bring one person to Christ, then ten new souls will be added, including perhaps their families. Imagine the potential increase in two, five, ten years!

Equipping and Empowering the Church for One+Plus+One

What will it take for the Yucaipa Church of Christ to effectively do ONE+PLUS+ONE? Consider the following:

Faith. The Hebrews writer stated, "Without faith, it is impossible to please [God], for whoever would draw near to God must believe that he exists and that he rewards those who seek him" (Heb. 11.6). Each person within the Yucaipa congregation must truly believe that God can do wonderful things through us.

Desire. Of course, the desire to get the job done is essential, not merely believing it can be done, but that we *desire* to do it. Numerical growth is not only a physical concern, but an emotional concern as well. Numerical growth, and the spiritual growth that equips it, means new people will come into the congregation, and that can be intimidating. Why? New people can upset the balance, and alter the sense of normalcy that some, perhaps many, cling to. In addition, spiritual and numerical growth is the Lord's work, but it *is* work. It can be hard and disappointing, to be sure; it can also be exciting and engaging.

Knowledge. God told Israel through Hosea, "My people are destroyed for lack of knowledge…" (Hos. 4.6). We need to become "people of the book," people who are diligent students of the Bible and who are willing to share that knowledge. The point is not that each member earns a master's degree in biblical studies, but each member learns how to strengthen and then share his or her faith, conviction, and desire for salvation. It is not learning the "plan of salvation," per se, but knowing the theme of the Bible as God's desire to save those who will come to him. As Peter encouraged the scattered churches, so then we should be encouraged as well: "...always being prepared to make a defense to anyone who asks you for a reason for the hope that is in you..." (1 Pet. 3.15).

The congregation can engage in a cooperative effort of study and learning through the classroom and the pulpit. Through such study and preaching, each family can be prepared through a discussion of the task before us, the methods of carrying out that task, and gaining the biblical knowledge necessary to be successful.

Cooperation. Of course, such a worthy endeavor will take cooperation within and among the congregation. We do not all have the same strengths, knowledge, and opportunities. For example, I have some knowledge and ability to study the Bible with people, but, as a newcomer to the community, I do not know very many people. Someone who has a long and strong association with the area may know hundreds of potential studies, but may not have the means by which an effective study can be done. So, I can be placed into a home, with the individual/family one of our families has targeted for evangelism. We have many members of this congregation who are both highly capable of conducting a Bible study *and* have a large network of friends, as well as family, within the community. The point is working together as a congregation and spiritual family seeking to share the Gospel.

Prayer. Paul wrote, "...be constant in prayer," rendered elsewhere as "pray without ceasing" (Rom. 12.12). Prayer is an essential element of success for any congregation, and for any program of church growth. Prayer becomes a personal and collective conversation with God, and that is so vital to any effort we make as a congregation of the Lord's church.

Conclusion

ONE+PLUS+ONE is not the final word on church growth, nor is it unique in any way. It is merely *one* way of growing spiritually and numerically. I will emphasize that our focus must be spiritual growth, for I believe that once we are growing spiritually, we will naturally begin to grow numerically because we cannot help but share what we know and have in our possession. The Gospel is a message of hope, and that is a valuable tool to give to this community. Imagine, just imagine, fifty percent of our families—one half—or more, working to bring one person per family into salvation. Imagine how much spiritually stronger we can become doing this. Crunch the numbers in your mind (and heart): each participating family seeking to bring *one* person into the Lord's church. It would be our version of the day of Pentecost; our re-creation of the conversion of Lydia, an Ethiopian treasurer, a Pharisee named Saul, four Athenian thinkers among the Areopagus, and so on.

The potential is limitless, but the work is critical. It *can* be done.

Bibliography

Allen, Joseph. "Renewal of the Christian Community: A Challenge for the Pastoral Community," *St. Vladimir's Theological Quarterly* 29 (January-March 1985): 305–323.

Anderson, Lynn. *They Smell Like Sheep: Spiritual Leadership for the 21st Century*. West Monroe, LA: Howard Publishing Co, 1997.

Armour, Michael C. and Don Browning. *Systems-Sensitive Leadership: Empowering Diversity Without Polarizing the Church*. Joplin, MO: College Press, 1995.

Balda, Janis Bragan and Balda, Wesley D. *Handbook for Battered Leaders*. Downers Grove, IL: IVP Books, 2013.

Banks, Robert and Bernice M. Ledbetter. *Reviewing Leadership: A Christian Evaluation of Current Approaches*. Grand Rapids, MI: Baker Academic, 2004.

Banks, Robert and Kimberly Powell, eds. *Faith in Leadership: How Leaders Live Out Their Faith in Their Work—and Why It Matters*. San Francisco: Jossey-Bass Publishers, 2000.

Barbuto, J. E. & Wheeler, D. W. (2006). Scale development and construct clarification of servant leadership. Group & Organization Management 31(1), 300–326. doi: 10.1177/1059601106287091.

Barna, George. *The Power of Vision*. Ventura, CA: Regal, 1992.

Barton, Ruth Haley. *Pursuing God's Will Together: A Discernment Practice for Leadership Groups.* Downers Grove, IL: IVP Books, 2012.

_____. *Strengthening the Soul of Your Leadership: Seeking God in the Crucible of Ministry.* Downers Grove, IL: IVP Books, 2008.

Bass, Bernard M. *The Bass Handbook of Leadership: Theory, Research, and Managerial Applications.* New York: Free Press, 2008.

Becker, Penny Edgell *Congregations in Conflict: Cultural Models of Local Religious Life.* Cambridge, UK: Cambridge University Press, 1999.

Beebe, Gayle D. *The Shaping of An Effective Leader: Eight Formative Principles of Leadership.* Downers Grove, IL: IVP Books, 2011.

Bjugstad, Kent. "A Fresh Look at Followership: A Model for Matching Followership and Leadership Styles." Institute of Behavioral and Applied Management, 2006. *Journal of Business and Management* 17.3, 2006. http://ibam.com/pubs/jbam/articles/vol7/no3/JBAM_7_3_5_Followership.pdf.

Black, David Alan. "The Pauline Love Command: Structure, Style, and Ethics in Romans 12.9–21," *Filologia Neotestamentaria* 2 (May 1989): 1–21.

Boa, Kenneth. *Conformed To His Image: Biblical and Practical Approaches to Spiritual Formation.* Grand Rapids, MI: Zondervan, 2001.

Bray, Gerald, ed. *Ancient Christian Commentary on Scripture: New Testament,* Vol. 6, "Romans"(Downers Grove, IL: InterVarsity Press, 1998.

Chaleff, Ira. "Courageous Followers, Courageous Leaders." New Relationships for Learning and Performance: Ideas for Leaders. December 2001. http://www.exe-coach.com/courageous-followers-courageous-leaders.htm

_____. "Leader-Follower Dynamics." *Innovative Leader* 12.8 (August 2003): 1–4.

Culpepper, R. Alan. "God's Righteousness in the Life of His People: Romans 12–15," *Review and Expositor* 73 (Fall 1976): 451–463.

Dale, Robert D. *Pastoral Leadership: A Handbook of Resources for Effective Congregational Leadership.* Nashville: Abingdon Press, 1986.

Drury, Sharon. *Handbook of Leadership for Church Leaders.* Regent University, 2003.

Dunn, James D.G "Romans 9–16," *Word Biblical Commentary*, Vol. 38 Dallas: Word Books, 1988.

Eims, LeRoy. *Be the Leader You Were Meant to Be: What the Bible Says About Leadership.* Wheaton, IL: Victor Books, 1975.

Elwell, Walter A., ed. *The Concise Evangelical Dictionary of Theology* (Grand Rapids, MI: Baker Book House, 1991.

Engstrom, Ted W. and Larson, Robert C. *Integrity.* Waco, TX: Word Books, 1987.

Fair, Ian A. *Leadership in the Kingdom: Sensitive Strategies for the Church in a Changing World.* Abilene, TX: ACU Press, 1996.

Ford, Leighton. *Transforming Leadership: Jesus' Way of Creating Vision, Shaping Values, and Empowering Change.* Downers Grove, IL: InterVarsity Press, 1991.

Gallagher, Dan. "Mark 10.45 Biblical leadership is servant leadership: Jesus came to serve…" *Truth or Tradition*.www.truthortradition.com/modules.php?name=News&file=print&sid =751.

Galindo, Israel. *The Hidden Lives of Congregations: Discerning Church Dynamics.* Herndon, VA: The Alban Institute, 2004.

Goethals, George R. and Sorenson, Georgia L. J., eds. *The Quest For a General Theory of Leadership.* Cheltenham, UK: Edward Elgar, 2006.

Guroian, Vigen. "Seeing Worship as Ethics: An Orthodox Perspective," *Journal of Religious Ethics* 13 (Fall 1995): 332–359.

Grayson, Don and Speckhart, Ryan. "The Leader-Follower Relationships: Practitioner Observations." *Leadership Advance Online* 6 (Winter 2006): 1–6.

Greenleaf. R. K. (1977). *Servant leadership: A journey into the nature of legitimate power and greatness.* New York: Paulist Press.

Gregory, Alyssa. "5 Steps to Effective delegation. *Sitepoint.* November 10, 2009. http://www.sitepoint.com/5-steps-to-effective-delegation.

Halverstadt, Hugh *Managing Church Conflict.* Louisville: Westminster/John Knox Press, 1991.

Haslam, Alexander and Reicher, Stephen D. "Leadership and Followership." *Vision* Winter 2008.http://www.vision.org/visionmedia/article.aspx?id=4744.

Hays, Richard B. *The Moral Vision of the Testament: A Commentary Introduction to the New Testament Ethics.* San Francisco: Harper-Collins Publishers, 1996.

Heller, Trudy and Van Til, Jon (1982). "Leadership and Followership: Some Summary Propositions," *Journal of Applied Behavioral Science* 18, 405–414.

Hesse, Hermann. (1956). Journey to the East. New York: Farrar, Straus, & Giroux.

Hogan, Norman. *Leadership in the Local Church.* Henderson, TN: Nakari Publications, 1988.

Howell, Don N. *Servants of the Servant: A Biblical Theology of Leadership.* Eugene, OR: Wipf & Stock, Publishers, 2003.

Huffard, Everett "Faith Development and the Church: Class Notes," *Harding University Graduate School of Religion* (Memphis, TN), 2003.

Jones, Jeffery D. *Heart, Mind, and Strength: Theory and Practice for Congregational Leadership.* Herndon, VA: The Alban Institute, 2008.

Kast, Fremont E. and Rozenzweig, James E. "General Systems Theories: Applications for Organizations and Management," *Academy of management Journal*, vol. 15, no. 4 (December 1972): 447–465.

Kelley, R. E. (1988) "In praise of followers." *Harvard Business Review* 66, 142–148.

_____. (2008). *Rethinking followership. The art of followership: how great followers create Great leaders and organizations* (1st edition). San Francisco, CA: Jossey-Bass.

Kotter, John P. *Leading Change*. Boston, MA: Harvard Business School Press, 1996.

Kouzes, James M. and Barry Z. Posner, *The Leadership Challenge: How to Get Extraordinary Things Done in Organizations*. San Francisco: Jossey-Bass Publishers, 1987.

Krishnan, Venkat R. "Leader-Member Exchange, Transformational Leadership, and Value System.

Kupers, Wendelin. "Perspectives on Integrating Leadership and Followership." *International Journal of Leadership Studies* 2.3, 2007, pp. 194–221. http://www.regent.edu/acad/global/publications/ijls/new/vol2iss3/kupers/kupers.htm

Ladd, George Eldon. *A Theology of the New Testament*. Grand Rapids, MI: William B. Eerdmans Publishing Company, 1974.

Latour, Lt. Col. Sharon M. "Dynamic Followership: The Prerequisite for Effective Leadership." 11–12-2013. http://govleaders.org/dynamic_followership.htm.

Laub, J. (2004, August). "Defining servant leadership: A recommended typology for servant leadership studies." Paper session presented at the Servant Leadership Roundtable, Regent University.

Lundin, Stephen C. and Lancaster, Lynne C. "Beyond Leadership…The Importance of Followership." *Futurist* 24.3 (May/June 1990): 18–22.

Luther, Martin. *Commentary on the Epistle to the Romans,* trans. J. Theodore Mueller. Grand Rapids, MI: Kregel Publications, 1976.

McGarvey, J.A. *A Treatise on the Eldership.* Chillacothe, OH: Deward Publishing Company, 2010.

Malphurs, Aubrey *Being leaders: The Nature of Authentic Christian Leadership.* Grand Rapids, MI: Baker Books, 2003.

Maxwell, John C. *Becoming a Person of Influence: How to Positively Impact the Lives of Others.* Nashville, Atlanta, London, Vancouver: Thomas Nelson Publishers, 1997.

_____. *Developing the Leaders Around You.* Nashville: Thomas Nelson Publishers, 1995.

_____. *The 21 Irrefutable Laws of Leadership: Follow Them and People Will Follow You.* Nashville: Thomas Nelson Publishers, 1998.

_____. *Thinking For a Change: 11 Ways Highly Successful People Approach Life and Work.* Warner Books, 2003.

Meilinger, Col Phillip S. "The Ten Rules of Good Followership." *AU-24 Concepts for Air Force Leadership.* Richard I. Lester and A. Glenn Morton, eds. Maxwell Air Force Base, AL: Air University Press, 2001.

Melander, Rochelle. *A Generous Presence: Spiritual Leadership and the Art of Coaching.* Herndon, VA: The Alban Institute, 2006.

Mercer, Don. "Followership: the Corollary to Leadership." *Todd Nielson: Leadership, Execution…Success.* March 20, 2012.

Morse, Mary Kate. *Making Room for Leadership: Power, Space, and Influence.* Downers Grove, IL: IVP Books, 2008.

Nayab, N. Edited by Ginny Edwards. "Servant Leadership- Strengths and Weaknesses." May 5, 2011.

Nikkel, James R. "Church Growth Leadership Theory and Mennonite Brethren Theology," *Direction Journal* 20.2 (Fall 1991): 72–88.

Northhouse, Peter G. *Leadership: Theory and Practice*, 5th edition. Los Angeles: Sage, 2010.

Oxford Illustrated American Dictionary (London, New York, Sydney, Moscow: DK Publishing, Inc., 1998.

Parsons, George D. and Leas, Speed B. "Creative Tension in Congregational Life: Beyond Homeostasis," in *Conflict management in Congregations*, ed. David B. Lott. Bethesda, MD: The Alban Institute, 2001.

Perkins, Bill. *Awakening the Leader Within: How the Wisdom of Jesus Can Unleash Your Potential*. Grand Rapids, MI: Zondervan Publishing House, 2000.

Pier, Mac. *Consequential Leadership: 15 Leaders Fighting For Our Cities, Our Poor, Our Youth and Our Culture*. Downers Grove, IL: IVP Books, 2012.

Pneuman, Roy W. "Nine Common Sources of Conflict in Congregations," in *Conflict Management in Congregations*, ed. David B. Lott. Bethesda, MD: The Alban Institute, 2001.

Prime, Jeanie and Salib, Elizabeth. "The Best Leaders are Humble Leaders," May 12, 2014. *Harvard Business Review*. http://hbr.org/2014/05/the-best-leaders-are-humble-leaders.

Renesch, John. *Leadership in a New Era: Visionary Approaches to the Biggest Crisis of Our Time*. San Francisco: New Leaders Press, 1994.

Richards, Lawrence O. and Hoeldtke, Clyde. *A Theology of Church Leadership*. Grand Rapids, MI: Zondervan Publishing House, 1980.

Sander, J. Oswald. *Spiritual Leadership: Principles of Excellence for Every Believer*. Chicago: Moody Press, 1994.

Schein, Edgar. (1992).*Organizational culture and leadership*. San Francisco, CA: Josey-Bass.

Sendjaya, S., Sarros, J. C., & Santora, J. C. (2008). Defining and measuring servant leadership behaviour in organizations. Journal of Management 45(2), 402–424. Retrieved from EBSCOhost.

Shawchuck, Norman and Roger Heuser, *Leading the Congregation: Caring for Yourself While Serving the People.* Nashville: Abingdon Press, 1993

_____. *Managing the Congregation: Building Effective Systems to Serve People.* Nashville: Abingdon Press, 1996.

Steinke, Peter L. *How Your Church Family Works: Understanding Congregations as Emotional Systems.* Bethesda, MD: The Alban Institute, 1993.

Stabbert, Bruce. *The Team Concept: Paul's Church Leadership Pattern or Ours?* Tacoma, WA: Hegg, 1982.

Stoessel, Horace E. "Notes on Romans 12.1–2: The Renewal of the Mind and Internalizing the Truth," *Interpretation* 17 (April 1963): 161–175.

Strauch, Alexander. *Meetings That Work: A Guide to Effective Elder's Meetings.* Colorado Springs, CO: Lewis and Roth Publishers, 2001.

Time Management Guide, 2002. "Effective delegation skill." http://www.time-management-guide.com/delegation-skill.html. 11/7/13.

Thrall, Bill, McNicol, Bruce and McElrath, Ken. *The Ascent of a Leader: How Ordinary Relationships Develop Extraordinary Character and Influence.* San Francisco: Jossey-Bass Publishers, 1999.

Townsend, Pat and Gebhardt, Joan."Followership: An Essential Element of Leadership." http://www.qualitydigest.com/dec97/html/townsnd.html

Van Velsor, Ellen, McCauley, Cynthia D., and Ruderman, Marian N. *The Center for Creative Leadership Handbook of Leadership Development*, 3rd edition. San Francisco: Jossey-Bass, 2010.

Walters, James Christopher. *Ethnic Issues in Paul's Letter to the Romans: Changing the Self-Definitions in Earliest Roman Christianity.* Valley Forge, PA: Trinity Press International, 1993.

Webster's New Collegiate Dictionary. Springfield, MA: G & C Merriam Company, 1973.

Wikipedia, the free encyclopedia. http://en.wikipedia.org/wiki/Delegation. October 31, 2013.

_____. http://en.wikipedia.org/wiki/Followership. November 1, 2013.

Wright, N.T. *The New Testament and the People of God.* Minneapolis: Fortress Press, 1992.

Wright, Walter C. *Relational Leadership: A Biblical Model for Leadership Service.* Carlisle, UK: Paternoster Press, 2000.

Young, Howard. "Rediscovering Servant Leadership." *Enrichment Journal: Enriching and Equipping Spirit-Filled Ministers.* http://enrichmentjournal.ag.org/200202/200202_032_serv_leader.cfm

*For a full listing of DeWard Publishing
Company books, visit our website:*

www.deward.com

www.ingramcontent.com/pod-product-compliance
Lightning Source LLC
Chambersburg PA
CBHW022101090426
42743CB00008B/681